How To Be
A Money Magnet

Denise M. Scott

Copyright © 2008 by Denise M. Scott

All rights reserved. No part of this book shall be reproduced or transmitted in any form or by any means, electronic, mechanical, magnetic, photographic including photocopying, recording or by any information storage and retrieval system, without prior written permission from Money Magnet, Inc. No patent liability is assumed with respect to the use of the information contained herein. Although every precaution has been taken in the preparation of this book, the publisher and author assume no responsibility for errors or omissions. Neither is any liability assumed for damages resulting from the use of the information contained herein.

This publication is designed to provide and authoritative information in regard to the subject matter covered. It is published with the understanding that the publisher and author are not engaged in rendering legal, accounting, or other professional service. If legal advice or other professional advice, including financial, is required, the services for a competent professional person should be sought. – From a Declaration of Principles, jointly and adopted by a Committee of the American Bar Association and Committee of Publishers.

ISBN 0-7414-4592-1

Published by:

INFINITY
PUBLISHING.COM

1094 New DeHaven Street, Suite 100
West Conshohocken, PA 19428-2713
Info@buybooksontheweb.com
www.buybooksontheweb.com
Toll-free (877) BUY BOOK
Local Phone (610) 941-9999
Fax (610) 941-9959

Printed in the United States of America
Printed on Recycled Paper
Published April 2008

Special thanks to my friend and colleague Kathy Chu. This book is possible because of her help and expertise with editing. Thanks, Kathy!

This book is dedicated to my parents, Esther and Elbert Mathis, who taught me how to save money, leverage credit, and walk in the prosperity of God. I will be forever grateful for your wisdom and the knowledge you imparted to me in life, especially regarding finance and credit cards. Thanks, Mom and Dad!

Introduction

Congratulations! You have taken the first step toward becoming a Money Magnet. What is a Money Magnet? It is a specific way to approach your personal finances to accomplish your goals, eliminate bad debt, create wealth, and attract money to you.

It is very sad to see people who worked diligently from age eighteen to age sixty-five be forced to retire with less than one thousand dollars in the bank. Experts say that when most Americans retire, they will be financially dependent on the government or on other family members. You can protect yourself from being dependent on the government and family members by preparing for your future and having a clear understanding of money. The problem is that most people don't understand money, how money works, how to accumulate money, and how to utilize it efficiently.

Let's start by understanding the definition of money. Money is only an object that represents the value of your efforts. Therefore, you are paid based on the value of your efforts. If you want to increase the amount of money you earn, you must first increase your efforts.

> Money is an object that represents the value of your efforts!

To increase your income from your job, start to think: how can I accomplish the tasks of my job faster or cheaper? How can I increase the bottom line or customer base for my company?

By intensifying your efforts, you become more valuable to your employer. Producing excellence in service to your employer equals more money in your pocket!

> Excellence equals more money!

Now that you understand the definition of money and how to increase your value, let's look at what happens when you receive money.

Once you receive money, you must decide what you are going to do with it. You can spend it, save it, or invest it. Whatever you decide to do with the money you receive, you will have to live with the consequences. What are you doing with your **money**?

Money is not for spending! Money is for giving, investing, saving, and spending — in that order! How can you give and invest your hard-earned money when you need every penny for your daily living expenses?

> Money is for giving, investing, saving, and spending!

You give and invest your hard-earned money by establishing a systematic approach. This book will outline practical applications to help you accomplish and measure your goals. As you read this book and apply the steps outlined to your daily life, you will begin to systematically eliminate bad debt, create wealth, and attract money to you.

> You give and invest your hard-earned money by creating a systematic approach!

You are well on your way to becoming a Money Magnet and being abundantly supplied.

Let's get started!

Table of Contents

Introduction i

How to Use This Book v

Chapter 1 1

Where is the Money Going? 2

How to Save Money While Shopping 12

Grocery Shopping 18

Car Shopping 22

Increasing Your Income 26

Banks, Banks, and More Banks 28

Paying Bills 33

Different Money Management Styles 36

Chapter 2 43

The Money Game 44

Creating a Cash Flow Spending Plan 76

Chapter 3 83

Plastic Money 84

Different Types of Debt 89

The Systematic Way to Eliminate Debt 92

Fallback Money 102

Increasing Your Credit Score Health 105

Chapter 4 121
Your Largest Investment 122

Chapter 5 127
Financial Fitness 128

Testimonials 133

Epilogue 137

Thank You 139

Appendix 141

References 153

How to Use This Book

This book is not a substitute for professional financial advice for your specific situation; however, it is a general guideline of financial principles.

The pages of this book are not only for your reading pleasure. They also provide a practical way for you to take action over a period of time. As you read each section and apply the financial principles you consider necessary for your life, you will begin to experience positive changes.

To get the most out of this book, you should read one chapter twice each day. After reading each chapter thoroughly, do the exercise. Be sure to complete it before you begin the next chapter. The chapters are concise, yet comprehensive and easy to read. If necessary, read each chapter with a highlighter in your hand, highlighting each section that you would like to refer to later. After you have thoroughly read each page of this book and completed all the exercises you deemed necessary, you can use it as a reference for any questions you may encounter later. Review it monthly for lasting benefits.

If you are in a hurry and prefer to take the fast path approach to accomplishing your goals, follow the outline below:

Fast Path Approach:

If your goal is to eliminate debt, read the section titled "The Systematic Way to Eliminate Debt" in Chapter 3.

If your goal is to have more money at the end of the month, read the section called "The Money Game" in Chapter 2.

If your goal is to understand credit cards, read the section named "Plastic Money" in Chapter 3.

Whatever your goals are, you can achieve them. Goal by goal and step by step, each goal begins with you taking the first step and then continuing to take one step at a time.

Chapter 1

Where is the Money Going?

Day 1

You are making more money today than you have in the past but still seem to have no money for savings. You seem more in debt than your parents and grandparents. Personal savings are at an all-time low. Where is all the money going?

The cost of housing has greatly increased over the last ten years. The average cost of a home is over $200,000. In addition to the rising housing cost, all other living expenses have risen, too; however, personal income has not kept pace with living expenses.

The average family with two children cannot afford to purchase a house and go on vacation every year. Families that do manage to save enough money to purchase a house and provide for their family will pay a high premium, not only in money but also in mental stress.

After these families purchase a home, they can no longer afford to continue to take family vacations once a year or treat their family to a fun night out to the movies once a week. Adventures such as these, which seemed to be staples in the family structure just a few short years ago, are definitely luxuries today. Where is all the money going? Income is paying for the higher cost of the basic necessities of food and shelter.

There is no extra money. There is no disposable income. And there is barely enough money to pay all the bills by the end of each month. Therefore, every detail of your financial life must be planned in advance.

> Plan the financial details of your life!

Most of the time, people allow money to hold them back from reaching their highest potential in life. Just think. If you had enough money to achieve any goal, what would you accomplish with your life? Take five minutes to think about what you want to do with your life financially. Be creative, yet realistic. Ideas to consider: increase your salary by $10,000 in the next twelve months, build a new home, or sell your house. Think of ideas that are important to you. You may want to make a list of some changes that could make your life easier financially, then start to narrow your ideas down to one specific financial goal.

A goal is a specific ideal to target, to learn from, to measure, and to achieve. This goal is the overall picture of your future. Once you have your specific goal in mind, visualize your goal completed. You and only you have control over your financial future.

> A goal is a specific idea to target, to lean from, to measure, and to achieve.

Life's goals are not accomplished by accident. When you achieve anything in life, it is the result of a well thought out action plan. In addition to an action plan, you will need to make a list of small daily tasks you will perform to help you reach your goal.

Small daily tasks are road maps that move you toward achieving your goal and bring you into the future you visualized.

Why use small daily tasks? It is easier to work on your goal in small steps then try to accomplish it all at once. You are the driving force. Make sure your goal is important to you. Ask yourself, "Why is this goal important?" You will accomplish your goal one step at time, task by task.

> Your life action plan is accomplished by completing small daily tasks!

By this time, you should have a specific goal in your mind. It is time to put your goal on paper. A goal is not a goal until it is acknowledged in writing. What is your goal? (Write your answer.)

_____
_____
_____
_____

What is preventing you from accomplishing your goal? Is it education? Money? Desire? Effort?

_____
_____
_____
_____

You wrote your goal and the obstacles that stand in the way of you achieving your goal. To turn your goal into reality requires you to define a series of small daily tasks to move you toward your future. The tasks are directions to identify what is required for you to accomplish each day to bring your goal to reality.

A **life action plan** had been provided for you to refer to at the end of this book. On your blank **life action plan,** write your goal. This should be the same goal that you wrote earlier. Now, think about all the tasks you must complete to accomplish this goal. Some tasks will be small and some will be large; however, break each large task down into smaller tasks so they can be completed daily. Write all the tasks you can think of today, and add additional tasks later as you move forward.

Number the tasks to complete in the order of importance. Once the tasks are numbered, write the tasks on your **life action plan**. These tasks are crucial for you to achieve your goal. In the column with the word "**Goal**," write your goal. In the blocks below, write one task per block. Make sure each task is small enough to be completed daily. Once your **life action plan** is complete, it should look similar to *Example 1: A Goal with Tasks* in this book. Additional blank life action plans are provided at the end of this book.

Life Action Plan:

Start Date	Goal:	Scheduled Completion Date	Actual Completion Date

Example 1: A Goal with Tasks:

Start Date	Goal: Sell my condominium in six months.	Scheduled Completion Date	Actual Completion Date
	Small Daily Tasks		
	-Self assessment of home		
	- Evaluate what items need to be fixed/upgraded in home		
	-Living Room		
	-Dining Room		
	-Kitchen		
	-Bedroom		
	-Bathroom		
	-Hallway		
	-Laundry Room		

Example 1: A Goal with Tasks is just that — an example. Therefore, ***Example 1*** does not show all the details that are required to sell my condominium. At the end of the book, you will find a completed ***Example 1*** with all the goals and tasks listed. If you need to see the level of detail, please take the time to review ***Example 1: A Goal with Tasks*** at the end of the book.

It is decision time. You need to make a commitment to accomplish the small tasks in your life action plan every day, without fail. Take a deep breath! Are you truly mentally prepared to move forward with your life action plan? In other words, are you ready to be successful?

How do you think your success will help others?

_____
_____
_____
_____

Don't worry about being successful; just concentrate on completing your tasks. You may not have all the required knowledge to complete your entire goal, but you must be willing to learn, to conduct your research, and to provide whatever else it takes to acquire the knowledge to complete each step daily. You must be willing to complete the tasks you outlined each day to produce the desired results to accomplish your goal. The mystery to success in life is to be eager to complete all work required, intellectually and efficiently.

> Make a commitment to complete the necessary tasks to accomplish your goal!

Each goal in life begins with you taking the first step. The first step is determining a goal and making a commitment to completing the daily tasks. Take time to review your goal. Read your goal from your **life action plan** aloud every day. It is time to add start dates to each of your tasks. The start dates will guide you through the process to begin each task. Once the **life action plan** is populated with the start dates for each task, your plan should look similar to *Example 2: Goals, Tasks with Start Dates* in this book.

Example 2: Goals, Tasks with Start Dates:

Start Date	Goal: Sell my condominium in six months.	Scheduled Completion Date	Actual Completion Date
	Small Daily Tasks		
6/5	-Self assessment of home	6/5	
6/6	- Evaluate what items need to be fixed or upgraded in home	6/6	
6/7	-Living Room	6/7	
6/8	-Dining Room	6/8	
6/11	-Kitchen	6/11	

A completed **life action plan** has been provided for you at the end of this book.

Please note that the scheduled completion date column will reflect the start dates since these tasks are to be completed daily. The actual completed date is the date you finished each task. On the date you finished each task, record the actual date you completed the task. This is a good way to stay on track and measure your success for each day.

Objectives of Chapter 1, Day 1:

- Definition of a goal
- Determine your goal
- Develop small daily tasks
- Complete a life action plan
- Be committed to the plan

Notes:

How to Save Money while Shopping

Day 2

Temptation is all around. We are enticed every day to purchase all types of merchandise by sales personnel, commercials, and advertisements. According to *Social Psychologist*, various techniques are used to motivate us to purchase things. Some common techniques used are "Door-in-the-Face," "Lowball," and "That's Not All." These techniques are usually used in commission-based businesses.

With the "Door-in-the-Face" technique, the salesperson asks you to purchase a large ticket item that you cannot afford. Of course, you refuse to purchase this item. At that point, the salesperson reduces the price of the item. Since the reduced price seems more reasonable to you, and it seems like the salesperson is compromising with you, you purchase the item. However, the salesperson wanted you to purchase that item at that reduced price. This technique is called "Door-in-the-Face" because the item has a hefty price that most people cannot afford. The salesperson knows you will refuse the higher price. Therefore, the salesperson reduces the price based on the commission that he or she desires to earn.

The "Lowball" technique is when the salesperson shows you the benefits of a product and gives you a base price. Once the salesperson sees that you are emotionally committed to the product, he or she will provide attachments or upgrades to the item. This will raise the price of the product. Most people who are emotionally attached to a product will purchase the product at any cost.

With the "That's-Not-All" technique, the salesperson shows you an item, tells you the price, and, while you are thinking about that purchase, the salesperson tells you about a special deal or discount. As you continue to think, the salesperson will offer another discount or an item for free to encourage you to purchase today. The discounts seem to never end until you say you will take the item.

Reread the different sales techniques until you have a clear understanding of them. Then go to a store of your choice to see if you can identify what technique the salesperson is using. Do not purchase any items. However, notice the specific technique the salesperson is using.

What sales techniques motivate you to purchase and why?

_____
_____
_____
_____
_____
_____
_____
_____

Now that you understand some of the sales techniques people use to motivate you to purchase an item, it is time to learn how to save money while shopping. What you purchase is an investment, regardless of the item. If you buy high-priced fashions, cars, and gadgets, then you are investing in items of low value. It is in your best interest to purchase items that will increase in value over time instead of decrease in value. You work hard for your money; you want to make sure you are getting the most out of every penny you have earned. You need to purchase clothing and cars, but you don't have to spend lots of money.

When buying clothes, shop at consignment shops, resale shops, outlets, discount stores, and search the sales racks of your favorite retail stores. Don't give up quality for a lower price. You can find designer clothes at a lower price. You may buy an item at a lower price point, but how long will the item last? Purchase the item that will last a longer time.

This is my story. I needed a pair of eyeglasses a few years ago. I decided to purchase a pair of designer frames. All of my friends told me to go to a cheaper place to get the frames, but I wanted designer frames. The initial cost of my designer frames was $450. These frames were of good quality, and the style would last at least eight years. I bought the frames, and they have stayed in style for six years so far. The funny thing is that every place I go, I receive compliments on my glasses. My initial investment was $450; however, since I kept the frames and replaced the lenses every two years, the cost of my frames will be $56.25 per year for eight years. The moral of the story: the longevity of the product will lessen the initial investment. Every item you buy is an investment.

> Buy high quality items to increase the longevity of the item and reduce cost!

When you are ready to shop for clothing for yourself or your family, take an inventory of the closet. Take all items out of the closet. Get three boxes. Label the first box *Give*, the second box *Keep*, and the third box *Throw Away*. The items that will go in the *Give* box are items that are too small but are in good condition and items that have not been worn in one year. The next box is for your *Keep* items. These are items that can be worn and are still in style. The last box is your *Throw Away* items. These items are stained or out of date. Sort the items into these three boxes. Discard all the items in the box labeled *Throw Away* immediately. Take the box labeled *Give* to your favorite charity. Keep all the items in the box that is labeled *Keep*. Take all the clothes out of this box and separate them into sets: a jacket and a matching skirt on one hanger, etc. Hang all of the clothes that match together in sets, professional clothes, business casual, and fun clothes.

> Hang clothes together in sets!

Once you have organized your entire closet, collect all your jewelry. Separate your jewelry into sets: earrings, necklace, and bracelet. In your kitchen, you may have zipper seal freezer bags. Put each set of jewelry in a freezer bag. Coordinate the jewelry with your clothing and hang each zipper freezer bag on the hanger with the matching clothes. Do the same thing with your hosiery, and hang your belts on the appropriate clothing with the hosiery and the jewelry all on one hanger. When you take an item out of your closet, you will have the clothing, the hosiery, and the jewelry coordinated and ready to wear. Place your shoes and handbag together, either on a hanging shoe bag or in a shoebox so they will be easy to find. After an item is worn, either place the item in the laundry or take it to the cleaners immediately. Then place the items back in the closet. This way, you are organized and save lots of time.

Notes:

You are almost ready to go shopping. Determine exactly which items you will need to purchase, such as one beige wool sweater. Make sure each item you want to purchase will match other items in your closet. Make a list of the items and colors you need to purchase along with the amount of money you are willing and can afford to spend for each item.

Clothes Shopping List:

Items to Purchase	Colors	Price Guidelines

A basic wardrobe for a woman should be built around basic colors, such as black, brown, blues, reds, and purples. You should have a skirt, a matching jacket, a coordinating jacket, matching pants, coordinating pants, two blouses, basic black shoes, a handbag, and gold or sliver jewelry to match. You will also need a coordinating sweater and shawl (if desired), scarf, and belt. With just these few items, you can create many different professional outfits. The same principles can be used when shopping for clothing for a man or for children. These principles will save you time and money.

Objectives of Chapter 1, Day 2:

- Understand the techniques salespeople use to motivate you to buy items today
- Understand what motivates you to purchase items
- Buy items of value and quality
- Get organized
- Go shopping

Notes:

_____
_____
_____
_____
_____
_____
_____
_____
_____
_____
_____
_____
_____
_____

Grocery Shopping

Day 3

Now that the closets are organized and clothing shopping is complete, it is time to go grocery shopping. You may want to shop at a farmer's market for fresh food, or you may want to comparison shop at an organic food store as well as traditional markets. I have found that some organic food stores are less expensive then traditional food stores. To save time and money, the Internet may be your best resource. If you don't have a computer, go to your local library to use their computer. It takes less time and no money to search and compare items on the Internet.

I do not recommend going from store to store to purchase grocery items. By the time you drive to all the stores to comparison shop, you will have spent all your expected grocery savings in gas. You can utilize the Internet to find and view sales circulars online and also print store and manufacturer coupons. Check your local newspaper for coupons and call the Consumer Affairs Office, which is the 1-800 number found on the back of your favorite product. Leave a comment about the product. In turn, the Consumer Affairs Department will usually supply you with coupons to encourage you to use more of their product and will put your name on the promotion list to receive coupons by mail throughout the year. A good practice is to purchase your items and call the Consumers Affairs Department on the same day to leave a comment. This way, you should receive coupons in the mail within ten days. Once you have coupons in hand, it is time to plan your meals for the week.

> Search online for coupons!

Tons of money can be saved when grocery shopping by planning ahead. The key to reducing cost at the supermarket is to plan meals for the entire week. When preparing the menu for the week, start with staples, such as rice, beans, pasta, homemade soups, bread, eggs, fish, and chicken. Don't forget to add snack foods throughout the day, such as fruit, crackers, and soup. You can also plan to eat leftovers for lunch. It is always good to get the children involved in the menu planning process. You may want to set aside one day per month when the children cook for the family. This could be fun and a great teaching tool as well. Foods you prepare and cook at home are less expensive and more nourishing then prepared frozen foods or fast foods. Buying a head of lettuce is less expensive then buying the prepared and washed lettuce.

> Build your menu around staples.

Buy household cleaning supplies, detergent, soaps, and toiletry in bulk and on sale once a month if you have a place to store them. If you don't have storage in your home, buy them on sale each week. Once you have created your menus for the week, create a grocery list, listing all the items you will need to prepare your meals for the week, including snacks. Check the pantry for items you have; this will ensure you don't miss any needed items. Eat before you go grocery shopping. Determine how much money will be spent on food for the week, and stick to the guidelines. Take coupons, your grocery list, and a calculator with you. Stick to your plan and only purchase items that are on your list and within your spending guidelines. Take only the amount of money that you plan to spend. Take cash, not credit cards, not debit cards, and not checks. You may copy the ***Daily Menu*** in this book to populate it for the week. Post your menu on your refrigerator. It is time to go grocery shopping.

***Daily Menu*:**

Day of the Week	
Breakfast	
Snack	
Lunch	
Snack	
Dinner	
Snack	

Objectives of Chapter 1, Day 3:

- Shop at Farmer's Markets
- Comparison shop at organic markets
- Comparison shop on the Internet
- Call the Consumer Affairs Department
- Look on the Internet for coupons
- Create a weekly menu around staples
- Involve the children with menu planning
- Create a grocery list based on the weekly menu

Notes:

Car Shopping

Day 4

So, you are in the market for a new car. Remember, never sacrifice a good quality car for a lower price, but you don't have to pay a high price for a brand new car, either. There is good news, according to edmunds.com. "In the month of September, dealerships receive cars for the next year. At that point, they get very anxious to sell the current year's cars." This provides a great opportunity for you to buy a current car at a discount with a factory warranty. These cars have not been titled or used. You will be the first owner of the car.

Do your homework before walking into any dealership. You should be armed with valuable information: know the make and model of the car you want; check the Kelly Blue Book prices on the Internet; go to the manufacturer's website to find the manufacturer's suggested retail price of the car. This price is on the sticker in the window of the car, as well. From the manufacturer's suggested price, start thinking about a price range to pay for this car. Always offer less then the manufacturer's suggested retail price, which is the standard price for the car with standard features. The dealer's profit is built into this price; therefore, you have negotiating room to lower the price.

Once you have decided upon a general price range of how much you would like to pay for this car, determine the down payment. Call several dealerships and tell them the make and model of the car you are looking for. Make sure you write down the salesperson's name. Also, let them know the price range you want to pay for the car. Only go to the dealerships that have the type of car and the price range you are looking for.

When you visit the dealership, do not take any money, credit cards, or your checkbook with you. You are there to complete your research before you make a purchase. Request to see the car and take it on a test drive. Request to see the purchase invoice for the car. Once you see the invoice, you can start negotiating down from that price point to $1,500 - $3,000 under the invoice price. The invoice price is a good starting point to begin negotiations; it is the price excluding incentives, which means that the dealer paid less then the purchase price for this car depending on what type of incentives they received. What this means for you is more negotiation room to lower the price.

Don't get me wrong. The dealer and the salesperson should be paid for their time and talents, but knowing the prices and what they represent empowers you to make better choices. If you can purchase the car for less than the invoice price, the dealership will still make a good profit on the sale of the car. Also, they make money on any upgrades, financing, and the service department. Be mindful of the type of sales techniques they are using to motivate you to purchase today! Review Day 2 in this book.

Now it is time to put your financing in place. The best place to seek a low interest car loan is through your credit union. Your credit union will provide guidelines for you to follow. If you are not a member of a credit union, search the Internet for one located in your area or inquire at your place of work. A lot of employers are associated with credit unions.

On the day you are ready to buy a car, arrive at the dealership with financing in place. When you arrive at the dealership with financing in place, you are in charge. It is time to start the negotiations. Start with an offer that is $1,500 - $3,000 below the invoice price. Once you and the salesperson have settled on the price, ask the salesperson if they can beat your interest rate or if there are any special offers or rebates to further lower your cost.

Most of the time, auto salespeople will sell the car based on the monthly price point. They will ask if you can afford $500 per month. However, if you have financing in place, you drive the sale, not the salesperson. This means you will know exactly what you are spending in interest and the total cost of the car. It does not matter if you can afford $500 per month if you have to pay for the car for eight years.

It is a good idea not to finance a car for more than four years. If you decide to stretch the payments for five or more years, consider the value of the car. The value of the car could be completely depreciated by the end of the loan. Also, ask yourself if you can afford that particular car. Do you have enough money saved for a substantial down payment? Can you afford to maintain the car? Can you afford to fill the car with gas weekly? Will you be able to continue to save money if you purchase this car? If you answered *no* to any of these questions, you should purchase a more affordable car.

It takes pristine credit to lease a car and only fair credit to purchase a car. When you lease a car, the monthly car payments are less expensive, but the car payments continue endlessly with leasing. After the lease, you will either be required to purchase that car or lease another car. It is a never-ending cycle. However, if you insist on leasing instead of purchasing a car, put the difference between the lease payment and the car payment in a high interest account each month so that at the end of your car lease agreement, you will have a substantial amount of money to purchase the car.

Objectives of Chapter 1, Day 4:

- Research before buying a car
- Secure a loan
- Negotiate the price for the car

Notes:

Increasing Your Income

Day 5

There are several methods to increase your income. The first method is to give ten percent of your income to charity. What? How can I do that? Giving opens doors for you.

My story: I decided I wanted to attend college many years ago. A young man who recently graduated from high school had the same desire, but he had no money. The funny part is that I did not have any money, either; however, I sent the little money I had to the college that he desired to attend in his name. He was very grateful for the opportunity to attend a small community college. Then doors began to open for me. I received a better job and was able to pay for my first two years of college in cash. I did not have to partake in student loans.

Would I have had the same opportunity to attend college and not acquire any student loans if I had not given? Well, I don't know. The point is that I did give to this young man, and more was given back to me. In Day 1, you learned that money is for giving first. Give ten percent of your gross income to someone in need. Watch to see what doors open for you.

The second method to increase your income is by decreasing your tax liability. Your employer offers pre-tax benefit Flexible Spending Accounts (FSAs), also called Health Savings Accounts and Expense Reimbursement Accounts. These accounts reduce taxable income when paying for medical expenses or childcare costs. You are allowed to deposit pre-tax dollars into these employer-sponsored programs. These deposits result in a lower taxable income. The funds deposited in these accounts may be used to pay for various medical expenses and dependant care costs. A drawback to using these accounts is that any deposited funds must be used to pay for expenses before the year's end or the money is lost. Your deposits for health, dental, and childcare costs are subtracted from your salary before federal, state, and Social Security taxes are deducted. Therefore, your taxable income and your taxes are reduced. You pay less in taxes and your actual income may be greater.

Another pre-tax benefit is your 401(k) retirement plan. A 401(k) plan allows an employee to save for retirement while deferring income taxes on the saved money and earnings until withdrawal. The employee elects to have a portion of his or her wages paid directly into his or her 401(k) plan.

You should invest the maximum amount allowed by your employer and/or not less than ten percent of your gross income. You should contact your employer to find out the details of your specific plan. These plans are designed to help you plan for retirement and lower your tax labiality. It is not how much money you make but how much money you keep that counts. Keep all you can legally!

> You are well on your way to becoming a Money Magnet by giving to others first, saving pre-tax dollars, and acquiring knowledge to make better choices!

Objectives of Chapter 1, Day 5:

- Give to charity
- Take advantage of pre-tax benefits

Notes:
_____
_____
_____
_____
_____
_____

Banks, Banks, and More Banks

Day 6

Is your bank meeting your needs? Most people utilize the same bank their family and friends use. In some cases, the bank you are currently using may not meet your current goals. You must determine what you want your bank to do for you. Do you want a high-interest savings account? Do you want good customer service? Do you want free checking? Do you want low or no fee checking and saving accounts?

Write your goals for your bank.

_____
_____
_____
_____

Make a list of five banks you want to conduct business with in the future. Interview a large bank, a small community bank, an Internet bank, one credit union, and one insurance company bank. Most insurance companies own a bank. The insurance company bank has competitive rates for savings and checking accounts. Call your insurance company to learn the types of products and services that are available to you.

These are some of the products and services your bank should provide:

1. No fee or low fee checking account
2. A high-interest savings account
3. No or low minimum balance fees
4. A no annual fee credit card
5. A low-interest credit card
6. Free ATM access
7. Free ATM card

8. No fee for transferring money to another banking institution
9. Free Bill Pay (Bill Pay is a way to authorize your bank to write a check to pay your bills on a specific day). Bill Pay will save you time and money (I will discuss this later in this section).

More then one bank may meet your banking needs. One bank may have a high-interest savings account. Another may meet your needs for a no fee checking account. The key is to pay little or no money for the services provided. You can use the *Bank Interview and Comparison Worksheet* provided in this book to conduct the interviews with each bank.

Bank Interview & Comparison Worksheet:

Banking Features	Bank 1	Bank 2	Bank 3	Bank 4	Bank 5
Name of Bank					
Checking Account					
Average Minimum Balance					
Monthly Balance					
Monthly fees associated with writing checks					
Transfer of funds fee					

Bank Interview & Comparison Worksheet Cont'd:

Banking Features	Bank 1	Bank 2	Bank 3	Bank 4	Bank 5
Service charge for ordering checks					
Overdraft protection					
Return check charge					
Interest bearing account: monthly interest %	Yes No	Yes No	Yes No	Yes No	Yes No
Service fee for checking account					
ATM & Debit Cards					
Free ATM card	Yes No	Yes No	Yes No	Yes No	Yes No
Free use of in-house ATM	Yes No	Yes No	Yes No	Yes No	Yes No
Free use of ATM at other banks	Yes No	Yes No	Yes No	Yes No	Yes No

Bank Interview & Comparison Worksheet Cont'd:

Banking Features	Bank 1	Bank 2	Bank 3	Bank 4	Bank 5
Monthly fees associated with ATM card					
Savings Account					
Minimum balance for savings account					
Interest rate %					
Fee for transferring funds					
Any fee associated with savings					
Online Banking					
Cost for online banking					
Bill Pay cost					
Certified check charge					
What bank best fits your needs?					

After the interviews, map the results you found for each bank back to your goals.

Select the best bank or banks that meet your goals. Open a checking account and a savings account. Your checking account should be an account to pay your bills only. A checking account is only a pass through account. All excess funds should be deposited into your high-interest savings account.

> Congratulations! You have a pass through account and a high-interest savings account!

Objectives of Chapter 1, Day 6:

- Engage a bank to meet your goals and objectives

Notes:

Paying Bills

Day 7

The easiest, most consistent method to pay your mortgage is systematically. Authorize your mortgage company to withdraw your mortgage payment each month from your checking account on the same date. Just make sure your mortgage payment is in your checking account on the date the withdrawal will be made. This will ensure your mortgage is never late, save you time, and could help increase your credit score (you will not be late with your mortgage payment). No more mortgage late fees or running to the post office to buy stamps or sending a payment by overnight delivery. You will reduce your costs and possess peace of mind.

The best way to pay your utility bills is by utilizing the Bill Pay service provided by your bank. Most banks offer free online bill payment to anyone who signs up for online banking. Don't be afraid of online banking. Banks will allow you to pay any vendor online electronically, or you can authorize the bank to write a check for you to your utility company deducted from your account. You provide the amount and authorize the date the check will be sent. This service is like having your own personal assistant. Stop writing checks and sending payments through the mail. This one step could save you approximately $15 per month, depending on how many checks you write and send each month. Think about it. A month's supply of checks costs approximately $20, stamps and envelopes cost approximately 42 cents per bill, and I am not going to calculate the time it takes to write each bill and take them all to the post office. If you don't have to purchase as many checks because you authorize your bank to write the checks each month for you, the cost of purchasing the checks has decreased each month and the cost of the amount of stamps you need to purchase each month has decreased as well, saving you approximately $180 per year.

In Day 5, you established a no fee or low fee checking account and a high-interest savings account. Go to your employer to have your paycheck deposited into your checking account each payday. After you have established direct deposit for your paycheck, contact the customer service department at your bank to let them know you would like to set up a monthly withdrawal from your checking account to your high-interest savings account. For example, on the 30th of each month, deduct $100 from your checking account (the pass through account) and deposit the money into the high-interest savings account. This is the most efficient way to save money consistently and systematically.

The amount that is deposited into your savings account should be at least ten percent of your net monthly income. An example: if you bring home $4,000 per month, the amount that is deposited into your savings account is $400 per month. Okay! Take a deep breath! That is only $20.00 per day for five days. Another way to look at it is this: if you make $20 per hour, the second hour of work each day is for your savings account (the first hour is for charity). Review Day 5: Increasing Your Income. You may think you cannot save ten percent of your net income; if so, start with a lower amount, such as $10 per week, which is $40 per month. The point is to start the process. If you never start the process, you will not establish a consistent way to save.

This book is designed to help you accomplish your goals, eliminate debt, create wealth, and attract money to you. Start systematically and consistently saving today, regardless of the amount saved. If you are not willing to save $40 per month, which is only $10 a week, then read the beginning of this book again until you are willing to accomplish the goal of saving consistently.

Objectives of Chapter 1, Day 7:

- Pay bills consistently and systematically
- Review Day 5: Increasing Your Income
- Save consistently and systematically

Take the time to write how you feel about saving money!

Different Money Management Styles
Day 8

When it comes to managing money, two things usually happen. The money patterns of your parents are repeated or you decide to go in a different direction and find your own money management style. As you proceed down the path of finding your own money management style, you find yourself in the same financial situation as your parents. This situation can be either good or bad. This happens because you usually carry the same fears and truths about money as your parents. Therefore, in this section, we will learn the strengths and weaknesses of the different money management styles. You will discover your money management style and how to enhance your style to serve you.

Money management styles are similar to personality types. However, there are many personality types and only three different money management styles. As we discuss the different money management styles, you will start to understand why you manage money the way you do. In other words, your money management style reveals your beliefs about money. From your beliefs about money, you develop your risk tolerance. Your risk tolerance is the key to the way you feel and what you believe about money. Emotions are the driving force for the way you manage money. Your risk tolerance and your emotions together identify your money style. Don't be concerned with changing your money management style. It takes a long time to change your money management style, but you will be able to enhance your money management style quickly after reading and understanding this section. Before reading this section, make sure all steps in Day 7: Paying Your Bills are complete.

People think that money can provide more control, power, or love. People fail to realize that money is only an object; money represents the value of your efforts. People who have lots of money are people who are solving problems. Solving problems takes a lot of effort. Review the Introduction section of this book.

Let's examine how money management styles are developed. In most cases, children are raised by parents or an adult. These parents introduce values, morals, and many types of beliefs. The beliefs that are introduced come from the parent's belief system and are passed down from one generation to another, and they are influenced by the era of the parents, as well.

My story: my parents were raised in the depression era. They had lots of siblings and there was little money. They believed they should save money for hard times. They lived through hard times and survived on very little. Regardless of the type of job they had, they always saved money. They modeled what they believed every day of their lives. This belief system was introduced to me. They taught me how to save money as a child. The reason my parents saved money was not to have great times but to shelter themselves from hard times. Why? Because they grew up in hard times and believed hard times were going to come.

Likewise, whatever your parents believed and modeled when you were a child is likely what you currently believe and model. It is a natural progression of how we learn as children, following in parents' footsteps. From your belief system, your reasoning takes place.

Why do you save money? In my case, the answer is that my parents saved money for hard times because hard times are going to come. My reasoning demonstrates the same reasoning as my parents. I save money just in case something goes wrong.

From the belief system, risk factors start to take shape in the mind. Therefore, I start to think that if I don't save money, hard times will come and I will not be prepared. The risk factor evokes my emotions, and I save money because of the emotion of fear.

To visualize the process of how money management styles are developed, see *Diagram 1.*

Diagram 1:

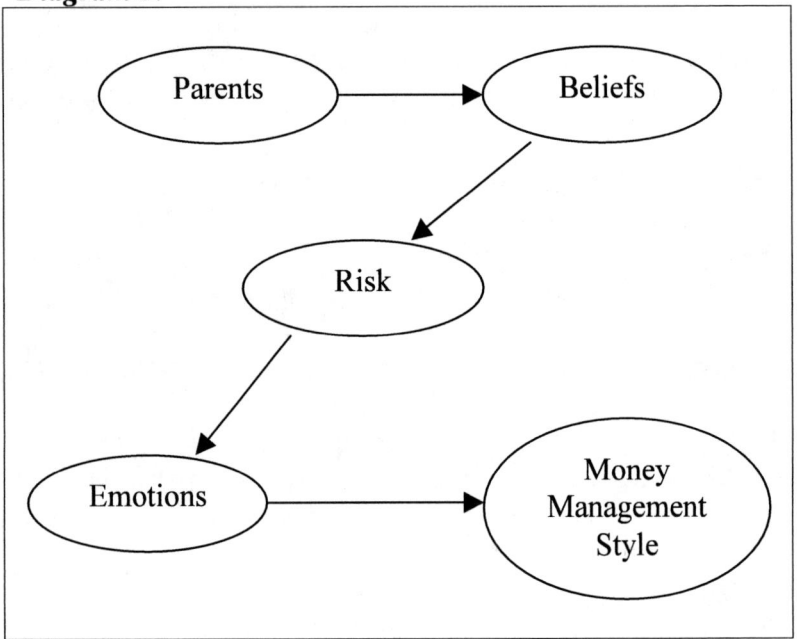

```
Parents  ───▶  Beliefs
                 │
                 ▼
               Risk
                 │
                 ▼
           Money
Emotions ───▶ Management
              Style
```

You may need to review this section until you fully understand the process of how money management styles are developed.

It is time to do some soul searching to find some answers. If you think you don't know the answers to these questions, ask your parents, your siblings, or someone from that era to help. Search your heart and soul, and be honest with yourself. Do not move forward until these questions are answered in full and you have a clear understanding of what you believe about money, what emotions are tied to your money management habits, and the beliefs of your parents.

What did your parents believe about money? What did they model?

_____
_____
_____
_____
_____

In what era were your parents raised? What did they believe?

_____
_____
_____
_____
_____

What is your belief about saving money? Do you save money or not? Why?

_____
_____
_____
_____
_____

What is your belief about saving money for a vacation? Do you plan vacations? Why or why not?

_____
_____
_____
_____
_____

Today, I save money for spending as well as for unforeseen events. I will discuss this in detail on Day 46, Chapter 3: Fallback Money.

Your money management style was introduced and influenced by your parents, yet you can create solid money management habits with a clear perspective and have your money style serve you well throughout your life.

There are three different money management styles. Each money management style can be successful. The styles are: Paycheck-to-Paycheck spender, the Good Life spender, and Money Magnet Living.

The characteristics of the Paycheck-to-Paycheck spender are that they spend all income; they find it more convenient to swipe a card then carry cash; they carry a credit card or a debit card. People in this group hide bills. They have no money to save. When emergencies arise, they are not prepared because they don't have savings and they spend all income. Their lives are filled with stress. Spenders feel good when they spend money, so they spend all the time to feel good. They love money because of the things money will buy them. This money style is high risk.

If you are a Paycheck-to-Paycheck spender, you should make sure your earned income is automatically deposited into your checking account each month. Each pay period, give ten percent to charity. The amount you give away will come back to you, not only in money but also in favor with other people. Create a systematic way to save. Review Day 6: Banks, Banks and more Banks, and review Day 7: Paying Bills, and apply these principles. After the principles are applied from Day 6 and Day 7, the remainder of the money in the bank is yours to spend as you please each month! Enjoy it. Later in this section, we will talk about Fun Money. This will be a principle you will want to apply as well.

The characteristics of the Good Life spender are that they use credit cards to spend more than they earn; they have more than one credit card; they carry a credit card balance on each card. They spend well over what they earn, and they are the masters of juggling money to try to beat a check to the bank before it bounces. Every month, they are always trying to figure out how they are going to pay their bills. They help make the banks and credit card companies rich because they pay late fees, over the limit fees, and bounced check fees. They are stressed each and every month. This money management style is very high risk. If you are a Good Life spender, you'll want to follow the same suggestions for the Paycheck-to-Paycheck spender. Also, you should stop using credit cards for one full year. This will help you gain control of your spending and stay on track.

The characteristics of Money Magnet Living are that the person is a saver; they don't like spending money for fun; they are very focused. They give ten percent of their money away. Savings is a priority in their life; therefore, they save a small portion of their income each pay period, and they invest a small portion of their income each pay period in their 401(k) and in a separate investment account. They live an enjoyable lifestyle. Savers use money and credit cards as a tool. They have credit cards to gain reward miles or some type of perks. However, they pay their credit card balance in full within ninety days or sooner. Savers are extremely creative with their money. This money management style is low risk. If you are a saver, you should follow these suggestions. Make sure all of your money is not in one basket. It you invest in stocks, you will also need to invest in real estate for balance. Balance is the key for savers. They need to spend some money for fun events. Later in this book, I will discuss Fun Money. This principle will also need to be applied as an outlet and balance.

Keep in mind that you are not trying to change your money management style. You are only applying the principles to help you be more successful with managing money. Regardless of your money management style, you can be successful by having a clear understanding of the characteristics of your style and enhance your methods of managing money. You may want to take the money management style challenge online. Just go to http://www.moneymagnetinc.com/personalfinance/moneystyles.htm.

What money management style are you?

_____
_____
_____
_____
_____

How are you going to enhance your style?

_____
_____
_____
_____
_____

Fun Money is five percent of your net income set aside for you and your family to have a fun activity. The only rule is that you must spend all the money in the fun account every pay period. If you spend all the money in one day, you will have to wait until the next pay period to have more fun and spend more money. Fun Money is for your enjoyment. Life is short. Start enjoying your life!

Objectives of Chapter 1, Day 8:

- Money management development
- Understanding your money style
- Enhancing your money style

Notes:

_____
_____
_____
_____
_____
_____

Chapter 2

The Money Game

Day 9

If you are like most people, you know what you are spending on living expenses but lack the knowledge of how much money is being spent at work or during time with friends. This first step in the money game is tracking spending. By tracking spending, you can determine where all of your money is going.

Every time you purchase an item, write down the date, the item bought, and how you felt before spending your hard-earned dollars to purchase the item. Write this information on your spending log for thirty-days. For example, if you go to the vending machine at work or school, write the amount spent in your spending log. If you play the lottery, write the amount spent in your spending log. If you smoke cigarettes, write the amount spent in your spending log. A spending log has been provided for you in this book. Use a separate piece of paper if additional pages are needed. A suggestion is included at the end of the spending log for each day. Allow the suggestion to guide you through the day. You may want to take the remainder of the day to think about the process before you begin.

Your thoughts:

_____
_____
_____
_____
_____
_____

Day 1 Spending Log (of 30 days):

Date	Item Bought	Need or Want	Cost	Feelings (money spent for item)

Create a shopping list before shopping!

Day 2 Spending Log (of 30 days):

Date	Item Bought	Need or Want	Cost	Feelings (money spent for item)

> Decide how much you will spend each day!

Day 3 Spending Log (of 30 days):

Date	Item Bought	Need or Want	Cost	Feelings (money spent for item)

Solve one problem today!

Day 4 Spending Log (of 30 days):

Date	Item Bought	Need or Want	Cost	Feelings (money spent for item)

Give a compliment to someone you don't know!

Day 5 Spending Log (of 30 days):

Date	Item Bought	Need or Want	Cost	Feelings (money spent for item)

Review your goals from Day 1!

Day 6 Spending Log (of 30 days):

Date	Item Bought	Need or Want	Cost	Feelings (money spent for item)

Keep your life action plan on track!

Day 7 Spending Log (of 30 days):

Date	Item Bought	Need or Want	Cost	Feelings (money spent for item)

Menu planning is key!

Day 8 Spending Log (of 30 days):

Date	Item Bought	Need or Want	Cost	Feelings (money spent for item)

> Determine one way to increase your income!

Day 9 Spending Log (of 30 days):

Date	Item Bought	Need or Want	Cost	Feelings (money spent for item)

Set up your Fun Money Account!

Day 10 Spending Log (of 30 days):

Date	Item Bought	Need or Want	Cost	Feelings (money spent for item)

Adjust your thermostat when you are not home!

Day 11 Spending Log (of 30 days):

Date	Item Bought	Need or Want	Cost	Feelings (money spent for item)

Unplug all appliances when not in use!

Day 12 Spending Log (of 30 days):

Date	Item Bought	Need or Want	Cost	Feelings (money spent for item)

Take your lunch to work!

Day 13 Spending Log (of 30 days):

Date	Item Bought	Need or Want	Cost	Feelings (money spent for item)

Spend your money in your Fun Money Account!

Day 14 Spending Log (of 30 days):

Date	Item Bought	Need or Want	Cost	Feelings (money spent for item)

Use coupons!

Day 15 Spending Log (of 30 days):

Date	Item Bought	Need or Want	Cost	Feelings (money spent for item)

Brew your own coffee or tea!

Day 16 Spending Log (of 30 days):

Date	Item Bought	Need or Want	Cost	Feelings (money spent for item)

Borrow DVDs from the library!

Day 17 Spending Log (of 30 days):

Date	Item Bought	Need or Want	Cost	Feelings (money spent for item)

Order prescriptions by mail through your insurance company!

Day 18 Spending Log (of 30 days):

Date	Item Bought	Need or Want	Cost	Feelings (money spent for item)

> Get your car repaired by a certified mechanic!

Day 19 Spending Log (of 30 days):

Date	Item Bought	Need or Want	Cost	Feelings (money spent for item)

Keep your vehicle tires inflated properly!

Day 20 Spending Log (of 30 days):

Date	Item Bought	Need or Want	Cost	Feelings (money spent for item)

> Follow the car manufacturer's recommendations!

Day 21 Spending Log (of 30 days):

Date	Item Bought	Need or Want	Cost	Feelings (money spent for item)

Save your bonus money!

Day 22 Spending Log (of 30 days):

Date	Item Bought	Need or Want	Cost	Feelings (money spent for item)

Buy on sale or in bulk!

Day 23 Spending Log (of 30 days):

Date	Item Bought	Need or Want	Cost	Feelings (money spent for item)

Treat yourself to lunch out today!

Day 24 Spending Log (of 30 days):

Date	Item Bought	Need or Want	Cost	Feelings (money spent for item)

Eat one meatless meal today!

Day 25 Spending Log (of 30 days):

Date	Item Bought	Need or Want	Cost	Feelings (money spent for item)

Treat yourself to a movie today!

Day 26 Spending Log (of 30 days):

Date	Item Bought	Need or Want	Cost	Feelings (money spent for item)

Buy quality clothes!

Day 27 Spending Log (of 30 days):

Date	Item Bought	Need or Want	Cost	Feelings (money spent for item)

Recite your goal aloud each day!

Day 28 Spending Log (of 30 days):

Date	Item Bought	Need or Want	Cost	Feelings (money spent for item)

> Call your telephone company to reduce your bill!

Day 29 Spending Log (of 30 days):

Date	Item Bought	Need or Want	Cost	Feelings (money spent for item)

Pay your bills by Bill Pay!

Day 30 Spending Log (of 30 days):

Date	Item Bought	Need or Want	Cost	Feelings (money spent for item)

Keep up the good work!

What have you learned about yourself?

_____
_____
_____
_____
_____
_____
_____

Are you more likely to purchase items that you need or want? Why?

_____
_____
_____
_____
_____
_____
_____

Objectives of Chapter 2, Days 9-30:

- Understand how money is spent with family and friends
- Understand your buying trends and feelings

Notes:

_____
_____
_____
_____
_____

Creating a Cash Flow Spending Plan

Day 40

The next step in the money game is creating a cash flow spending plan. Your cash flow spending plan is an analysis of how you run your household. This is a plan that can be adjusted to your needs and lifestyle. Your plan will tell you where you stand financially. You will need to decide what changes need to be made in your cash flow spending plan.

You will need your checkbook register or an online copy of your checks, a copy of a recent pay stub, and all of your bills (utility bills, credit card bills, mortgage, etc.) to complete this section. If you prefer to complete this section on your computer, log on to our website at http://www.money-magnetinc.com/personalfinance/elearning for an electronic version of the Cash Flow Spending Plan worksheet. The electronic version will generate and calculate the results for you. You can also complete the worksheet provided in this book manually. Just populate all the information in the left column first and add all the totals together, excluding the income total. Use the remainder of this day to locate all the items needed to complete this section. After you locate all the items, this section will take approximately one hour to complete.

Notes:

_____
_____
_____
_____
_____

Day 41

Cash Flow Spending Plan Worksheet:

Your Monthly Net Income	$		
Spouse	$		
Alimony & Child Support	$		
Total Income	$		
Mortgage/Rent	$		
Homeowner's Insurance /Renter's Insurance	$		
Property Taxes	$		
Electricity	$		
Gas	$		
Water	$		
Trash	$		
Lawn Care/Yard Work	$		
Total	$		
Car Payment	$		
Maintenance	$		
Gas	$		
Insurance	$		
Public Transportation	$		
Total	$		
Groceries	$		
Restaurant	$		

Cash Flow Spending Plan Worksheet Cont'd:

Take out food/fast food	$	Credit Cards	$
Total	$	Credit Cards	$
Clothing/Children	$	**Total**	$
Clothing/Adults	$	Student Loans	$
Clothing/Dry Cleaning	$	Personal Loans	$
Laundry	$	Line of Credit	$
Total	$	Miscellaneous	$
Prescriptions	$	Miscellaneous	$
Co-payments	$		$
Total	$	**Total**	$
Entertainment/Tennis/Golf	$	**Total Expenses** (Add all the totals together excluding the Total Income)	$
Movie/Game Rentals	$	**Total Income** minus Total Expense) minus the Total Income Line from your **Total Expenses line**)	$
Education/Children	$		
Daycare	$		
Babysitter	$		
Total	$		
Cable/DSL	$		
Internet	$		
Cellular Telephone			
Telephone (LAN Line)	$		
Total			

Do you have money left at the end of the month (Total Income minus Total Expense)?

_____
_____
_____
_____
_____

Are you satisfied with your results? Why or why not?

_____
_____
_____
_____
_____

How will your results assist you with completing your life action plan goal?

_____
_____
_____
_____
_____

How do you plan to change your results?

_____
_____
_____
_____
_____

Historically, housing is where most of your income is spent. As a guideline, you should spend between 35 and 45% of your total income on housing. If your housing cost exceeds these guidelines, don't fret. Just begin to identify other areas in your spending plan that can be reduced. The truth of the matter is that if there is no money left at the end of the month, you need to concentrate on decreasing your variable expenses. These are expenses that change each month, such as your utilities, telephone bills, credit card bills, etc. Create ways to cut back on expenses that you can control. You may want to install a programmable thermostat to help regulate the temperature in your home. You may want to purchase energy-efficient light bulbs to save on your utilities. You may want to disconnect your cellular telephone if you have a LAN line or cancel your cellular telephone service and use only your LAN line. You may want to limit the number of times you go out to eat. Maybe you can eat out only once a month instead of three times a month. Review Day 9: The Money Game in Chapter 2. Determine what you spend while with friends or family that you can reduce. The best and most efficient way to cut back is to drill down your credit card debt. We will discuss eliminating debt in a later section.

You may also consider increasing your cash flow. You can sell items online. Sell items from your home at a yard sale. Other people will buy items you don't want or no longer like. How does the saying go? "One man's trash is another man's treasure." You can utilize the different sales techniques you learned on Day 2 to motivate the consumer to purchase your goods. You could start a babysitting service. This service is especially needed during holiday time. Parents would love to go shopping without their children, but they have no one to care for them. Desktop publishing may be your forte; you can complete each task on a part-time basis in the comfort of your own home. Maybe starting a virtual assistance secretarial service is more suitable for your personality. If you prefer the outdoors, landscaping or delivering the local newspapers may work best for you.

Before leaving this section, you must have money left at the end of the month. It could be as low as $1.00, but you must have something left over. Stay with this section until you can either reduce your expenses or increase your cash flow and have at least $1.00 left at the end of the month. Although I don't suggest getting a second job, you can find another job until you can decide on a creative idea to increase your cash flow.

Objectives of Chapter 2, Days 40-41:

- Create a Cash Flow Spending Plan
- Adjust Cash Flow to meet your needs

Notes:

Chapter 3

Plastic Money

Day 42

How many credit card offers do you receive each month? According to experts, each household receives an average of six credit card offers each month. The average person has more than seven credit cards in his or her wallet. They have the "charge, please" plastic money "give it to me now" syndrome. You can have anything you want today, without waiting or paying for the product or service.

Credit cards are financial instruments that can be used over and over again to buy products, services, and borrow money. Basically, banks, retail stores, and other businesses issue credit cards. Buying items on a credit card and paying for them over a period of time is nothing new. In the 1800s, people who sold goods and services on installment plans were called tallymen. The trend of allowing a person to buy items on an installment plan grew since the numbers showed that the installment plan or credit card customer spent more money when they were allowed to pay on credit over time. The average amount of money spent with a credit card is 14% more than when cash is used.

According to statistical data provided by Creditcards.com, the first universal credit card was the Diner's Club card. It was introduced in 1950. This card was known as the travel and entertainment business card. The Diner's Club card had an annual fee, and customers had up to sixty days to pay the bill in full. In 1958, American Express launched their credit card, which was similar to the Diner's Club card. The first bank to allow universal revolving credit was Bank of America. In 1959, universal interest, late fees, and transfer fees were introduced to the public. Today, the credit card industry receives more then $43 billion in fees.

The charge card is a household name. And the words "charge, please" seem to be magic and a way of life. When you say the words "charge, please," what are you really saying?

You are saying yes to delayed payments and increased interest for goods and services provided today. You are saying yes, you can be trusted to pay the bill in full for the items or services provided. You are saying yes to sacrificing your life to have the items, goods, and services you want today before the money is earned.

> The credit card industry receives more then $43 billion in fees!

Credit cards are a short-term vehicle for short-term debt. Credit cards were never designed for long-term debt. If you cannot pay for an item in thirty, sixty, or ninety days, don't charge the item. If you are working your way out of debt, you should not charge any items at all. By using credit cards as long-term vehicles, you are putting yourself under unnecessary pressure and stress. The pressure and stress comes when the bill is due and there is no money to pay the minimum payment. Debt is, reportedly, the number one argument between all couples.

> Initially, credit cards were paid in full within sixty days!

In today's society, plastic money also consists of telephone cards, gift cards, and prepaid credit cards. This type of plastic money is paid for in advance of charging an item or service. If you feel an urge to charge, buy one of the prepaid cards and charge only five to ten percent of your net monthly income.

Locate all your credit cards and debit cards. In order to change your spending habits and become debt-free, drastic changes need to be made. Cut up all of your credit cards and debit cards and throw them away. If you find this step difficult to accomplish, you must decide if you are truly ready to get out of debt. You cannot get out of debt and continue to charge on your credit cards. As an alternative, put all of your credit cards, including your debit cards, in a plastic zipper bag. Fill this bag with water and place the bag in the freezer.

Many people ask me why I suggest destroying or freezing the credit and debit cards. The truth is, if you decide to purchase an item that is not on your cash flow spending plan, retrieving the cards will force you to think twice about the purchase. You should ask yourself: Is the purchase I want to make a necessity or a desire? Why am I buying this item? After asking yourself these questions and you still want to buy the item, buy the item with cash! Don't use a check! Use cash! By using cash, you make a decision to drain or not drain your available funds.

My story: When I was working my way out of debt, destroying my credit cards was the hardest step to accomplish. I depended on my credit cards as my emergency fund, and my debit card was a way to get cash quickly if I needed to buy something or just wanted to go out to eat. Credit and debit cards were my lifelines. I thought I could not live without them. It actually took me seven days to cut up my credit cards because I was so very attached to them. Once I made the decision to be debt-free and destroyed my cards, I immediately felt a sense of control.

How does this step make you feel? Why?

_____
_____
_____
_____
_____
_____

Review Day 8. What is the worst thing that would happen if you destroyed your credit cards?

_____
_____
_____
_____
_____
_____

What is the best thing that would happen if you destroyed your credit cards?

_____
_____
_____
_____
_____
_____

How does your decision to destroy or not destroy your credit cards affect your life action plan?

_____
_____
_____
_____
_____
_____

What have you learned about yourself?

_____
_____
_____
_____
_____
_____

Based on the information you learned in this section, how should credit cards be used?

_____
_____
_____
_____
_____
_____
_____

Review Days 9-41 and don't move forward until the steps in this section are accomplished.

Objectives of Chapter 3, Day 42:

- Plastic Money: what it is and how to use it
- Facing fear and getting spending in line

Notes:

_____
_____
_____
_____
_____
_____
_____
_____
_____
_____
_____
_____
_____
_____
_____

Different Types of Debt

Day 43

Debt in itself is not a bad thing. When you purchase items that appreciate in value, your debt is considered good debt. Acquiring an education is good debt. Higher education brings, in most cases, a higher paycheck, which allows you to pay off your bills and live a better lifestyle. Buying a home is good debt. A home provides shelter for you, and the home grows in value over time. If you decide to sell your home, you can buy a larger home using the value of your current home with little or, in some cases, no money needed.

When you purchase items that depreciate in value, debt is the result. Debt is a vehicle that uses your future purchasing power before the money is earned. When you purchase items that deprecate in value, your debt is considered bad debt. Clothes and cars, although they are necessary items, are considered bad debt. When you decide to use your credit card to buy expensive clothing and you know you are going to pay for these items over time, you are mortgaging your life, your family's lives, and your future by paying more for the items than the items will be worth when paid in full.

Debt is owing another person or company, either in money or service. Most people think they are not in debt if they can pay their bills on time. I was under that same false assumption. If you owe anything to anyone, you are in debt. The question to ask is this: is the debt good or bad?

> Good debt is purchasing items that appreciate in value!

A person cannot live life without some debt. How much credit card debt is reasonable? As a rule of thumb, your credit card debt, which is bad debt, should be between 5% and 10% of your net income. Too much bad debt can send you on the path to poverty. According to experts, the average impoverished person living in America has a nice home and has a car. They may also have the ability to pay the minimum monthly payment on their credit cards, but they still owe thousands of dollars to credit card companies. They work every day. The harder they work, the more they spend; the more debt they accumulate, the more they work. What a vicious cycle. Poverty is not having enough money to pay for basic living expenses and other items needed for survival, such as food and clothing. Whatever the amount of debt you have, you own it. It is your investment, regardless of whether it is good or bad debt. It is yours.

How much bad debt do you own?

_____
_____
_____
_____
_____
_____
_____
_____
_____

How much good debt do you own?

_____
_____
_____
_____
_____
_____
_____
_____

Objectives of Chapter 3, Day 43:

- Definition of debt
- Definition of poverty
- Good debt versus bad debt
- Determine the amount of your debt

Notes:

The Systematic Way to Eliminate Debt

Day 44

It has been established that bad debt consists of items purchased that do not appreciate in value. Review Day 43. The average person has a revolving charge balance on their credit card averaging $10,000.

My story: I used to spend nearly every cent I had, and when there was not enough money, the credit card became my lifesaver.

Are you like that? Most people don't pay off their credit card balances every month, and debt begins to build. It is no wonder that the old saying, "I owe, I owe, so off to work I go," is popular. The saying is true. Have you every felt compelled to show up at work sick? I have. I felt I needed my job because I had so many bills to pay. Ask yourself what would happen if you were laid off tomorrow. How would all of the bills be paid? How long would you be able to live on your savings? Do you have savings?

If you have been working for more then twenty years and are making at least twenty dollars an hour working forty hours a week, how much money do you have in your bank or investment account to show for all your time in the workforce?

_____
_____
_____
_____
_____
_____
_____

It is not how much income you make each week but how much income you keep that counts.

Why do you use credit cards?
_____
_____
_____
_____
_____
_____

Getting out of debt is more time consuming than accumulating debt. Let's start the process of debt elimination. Incur no new debt. Let me be very clear. Don't use any charge or debit cards. Review Day 42-43 and follow the corresponding steps before moving forward.

Gather all your credit card bills. You will also need your calculator, a pencil, a notebook, and a highlighter. Highlight any interest rate that is 10% or higher. Call each credit card company's customer service department to request a reduction in interest rate. Below is an example of a typical conversation.

You: "I am calling regarding account number 123456. My name is Denise. I am the cardholder. I would like to continue paying my bill on time each month, but I am finding it more and more difficult to pay because my interest rate is 30%. Therefore, I am requesting a lower interest rate of 20% (request 5%-10% lower). How can you help me?" (At this point say nothing at all. If the telephone goes silent, let it.)

If the credit card company's customer service department agrees to reduce your interest rate, you have accomplished your goal. If they say they cannot help you, ask to speak to the manager. Tell the manager you are seeking a reduction in your interest rate because you are having a hard time paying your bill. Then be silent. When there is silence in a conversation, that usually means a person is under some pressure to provide an answer. Most likely, you will receive a reduction in your interest rate. If a lower interest rate is denied, make a note in your book of the date, the time of the call, the reasons why the request was denied, and the name of the person to whom you are speaking. In three months, make the same request.

Credit card companies are in business to make money. Interest rates and fees are seen as profit centers to increase their bottom line. And guess who is giving the credit card companies the money? You! You can take the time to make one telephone call to the credit card company customer service department to request a reduction in your interest rate. This one step can save you thousands of dollars in interest payments.

Do you know how your interest rate is calculated? Don't worry, you don't have to calculate anything, but you will need to have a clear understanding of the method your credit card company is using to calculate your interest rate. The method to calculate your interest rate can save or cost you money each month. The best method to calculate interest is the Adjustable Balance Method (ABM). The balance is adjusted for any payments made; then the purchases are added to the adjusted balance and multiplied by the interest rate. This method results in a lower interest rate. What calculation method is your credit card company using? This information will be on your invoice from the credit card company, or you can contact them by telephone to ask.

Most credit card companies use the Average Daily Balance (ADB) method. With this method, the balance owed is divided by the days in the billing cycle, then multiplied by the interest rate. This method results in a slightly higher interest rate. If your credit card company is using the ADB method, you should pay your bill in full as soon as possible or pay half of the bill twice a month but before the due date. This will help reduce your interest paid.

Write down all of your credit card debts from the smallest debt to the largest. Write the starting balance of each debt and write the minimum payment of each debt. When you start reducing your debt, your assets could increase. Therefore, you are trading bad debt for assets. Assets are items that increase in value over time.

My story: When I was working my way out of debt, I contacted many credit counselors. They all told me I had to have additional money to work my way out of debt, but I was only making $29,000 per year and did not have one red additional penny to pay toward my debt. I started saying, "I have to find some money to help me pay down my debt." Therefore, I worked on reducing my interest rate.

As I freed up some cash (which I call Found Money) from the reduction of the interest rate, I applied that money to the minimum amount of debt I had.

Day 45

Let's take some time to talk about other ways to find Found Money. What is this thing called Found Money? It is money you have, but it is allocated to something else. Found Money could be money that you spend on lunch every day, or the extra money you may be paying to purchase pharmaceutical products at the local drugstore instead of purchasing these items through the mail with your insurance company. Found Money could be the money you are spending on late fees or Automatic Teller Machine fees. You could be paying for checks you are writing instead of using Bill Pay. You could be paying for food club fees that you don't use. Everyone has Found Money. Take the time to find your Found Money. Do not get your Fun Money and Found Money confused. Fun Money is money to use as you please for fun. It is not Found Money. Review Day 8.

Make a list of your Found Money. Add a monetary value to it.

_____
_____
_____
_____
_____
_____
_____
_____
_____
_____

Add up your Found Money. How much Found Money do you have? On a monthly basis, how much of your Found Money are you willing to add to help you pay down your debt? Give an amount that you can be consistent with every month.

If you have searched for Found Money and you truly cannot find any Found Money in your life, you can pay your credit cards twice a month, paying half of the amount owed on the first of the month and the other half of the amount owed at the end of the month but before the due date. For example, if your bill is due on the 15th of the month and the amount due is $100, pay $50 on the 16th of the previous month and pay the other $50 before the 15th of the month due. This way, you will pay less interest.

Found Money will help you reach your goal of debt elimination faster. Decide on an amount that you can consistently apply toward your debt each month. One credit card at a time will be paid off. Therefore, the Found Money will be applied only to your first credit card along with your minimum payment. For the other credit cards, the minimum payment will be sent to the credit card company.

Determine how long it will take to pay off your first credit card with your Found Money. To do this, take the total amount owed on the credit card and divide by the minimum payment, adding together your Found Money. Example: total amount owed is $500. The minimum payment is $50 and the Found Money is $50. Divide $500/$100 = 5 months to pay off this credit card.

Determine how many months it will take to pay off your first credit card with your Found Money. Follow the method explained.

_____
_____
_____
_____
_____
_____
_____
_____
_____

Once your first credit card is paid, add that money to the next credit card and include the minimum payment for that card. Example: the first credit card was costing $100 each month. The second credit card total balance is $1,000. The minimum payment for the second credit card is $100. Add the $100 from the credit card that is paid (this amount is your new Found Money). Divide $1,000/$200 = 5 months to pay off the second credit card.

Determine how many months it will take to pay all your credit cards with your Found Money. Follow the method explained.

_____
_____
_____
_____
_____
_____
_____
_____

Add up all the months and divide the months by 12 to find how many years it will take to get out of debt.

___

Determine the timeframe to pay off your first credit card paying the minimum payment only. Follow the method explained using only the minimum payment.

___

Add up all the months and divide the months by 12 to find how many years it will take to get out of debt paying the minimum payment.

___

Concentrate on paying down one debt at a time while sending the minimum payment to other credit cards, one at a time until each card is fully paid. Your Found Money makes the difference. The more money you find and can consistently apply toward your debt, the faster you will be able to eliminate your debt. When complete, look at how long it will take you to get out of debt if you only paid the minimum payments.

Notes:

Yes, there are other ways to eliminate debt. You can make a settlement with your credit card companies and pay less than you owe. If you would like to utilize this method, call the credit card company to let them know you are having trouble paying your bill. Tell them you want to make a settlement to pay your debt for 30% of what is owed. At this point, they will say one of three things: they will accept, they will deny, or they will make a counter offer. If your offer is accepted, the credit card companies will most likely want the entire amount agreed upon within thirty days or the agreement is terminated. Also, the fact that you did not pay the full amount of your debt will most likely be reported to the credit-reporting agency. In addition, the credit card company could send you a 1099 form at the end of the year for the amount of money that was not paid, which means you will owe taxes on the amount that was not paid.

Debt consolidation is also an option. Debt consolidation involves opening a loan to cover all your debts. This way, you have one bill. The concern with this option is that you will pay a smaller amount of money per month, but you will pay this debt for a longer amount of time, which means you will be paying more money over time. The other concern is that most people who use the debt consolidation option to eliminate debt usually find themselves in more debt less than two years after the date they opened the loan.

Bankruptcy should be your last option. To find out if you qualify for this option, see your attorney. If you qualify for this option, the bankruptcy could be reported on your credit report for ten years.

Which option will you choose?

_____
_____
_____
_____

Objectives of Chapter 3, Days 44-45:

- Systematically eliminate debt
- Pros and cons of other debt elimination options

Notes:

Fallback Money

Day 46

Fallback Money is money for miscellaneous expenses, such as oil changes, car inspections, plumbing, etc. This is also the place where I save for a yearly vacation; however, in this example, the vacation is excluded. Usually, people will not put money aside for miscellaneous expenses that do not occur every month. Most of the time, these expenses are forgotten. Thus, when these expenses arise, people will fall back on credit cards instead of having money set aside.

The good news is that these types of expenses **will not** take a chunk of money out of your pocket each month. Determine how much money you actually spent last year for oil changes, car inspections, plumbing, etc. You can also review your Cash Flow Spending Plan for items that don't occur every month. Below is the actual amount I spent.

Example of Yearly Fallback Expenses:

Misalliance Expenses	**Cost per Year**
Oil Change	$80
Car Inspection	$100
Plumbing	$200
Total for the year	$380

Divide the cost per year by 12 months = cost per month therefore, $380.00/12=$31.67

Follow the steps and create your Fallback Expenses.

Your Fallback Expenses:

Miscellaneous Expenses	**Cost per Year**

Once you have determined the amount per month that is needed to satisfy your miscellaneous needs, open a savings account designated as your Fallback Money Account. Every month, deposit that amount. Better yet, request your bank to automatically deposit that amount of money into your Fallback account every month from your checking account. Record every deposit and every withdrawal into this account.

Fallback Money Account:

Fallback Money Account	Deposit	Reason for withdrawal	Amount withdrawn	Total Amount
Deposit 6/1	+31.67			$31.67
Deposit 6/8	+31.67			$63.34
Deposit 6/15	+31.67			$95.00
Deposit 6/22	+31.67			$126.68
Deposit 6/29	+31.67			$158.35
		Car Inspection	-$100.00	$58.35

Your Fallback Account:

Fall Back Money Account	Deposit	Reason for withdrawal	Amount withdrawn	Total Amount

Objectives of Chapter 3, Days 46:

- Establish a Fallback Money Account

Notes:

Increasing Your Credit Score Health

Day 47

The most important method for maintaining and improving your credit score health is by paying bills on or before the due date. More than a third of your credit score is based on how bills are paid. If a bill is paid late, it does not mean that you are doomed. Call the creditor and explain your situation; then make payment arrangements and send the payment on or before the due date. Creditors are willing to work with you to resolve any payment issues, but you must comply with any new payment arrangements. If this is the first time your payment has been late, the creditor could provide the courtesy of not applying a late fee. After all, creditors are in business to make money and keep you as a customer. Therefore, ask the creditor not to apply the late fee.

Another portion of your score is based on how much you owe each creditor. The rule of thumb for credit cards and installment loans is to stay below forty-five percent of the credit limit. If you have a credit card and your credit limit is ten thousand dollars, never charge more than four thousand five hundred dollars at any time. If your debt is currently more then forty-five percent of your credit limit, you can call the creditor and ask to have your credit limit increased. If you are not in a financial position to increase your credit limit, systematically pay down debt and do not move your debt around to a zero percent credit card. The older your credit cards are, the higher your credit score. If you have a lot of newer credit cards, this will lower your score because there is no payment history for those credit cards. If you are maintaining your minimum monthly payments and you are at your credit limit on one or more credit cards, you are at greater risk of getting in over your head. This will be reflected in your score.

By systematically paying down debt and not increasing debt, you will increase your credit score in two areas: payment history and amount owed. These areas consist of more than half of your credit score.

Each time you apply for credit, you lose points on your credit score. A good rule of thumb is to keep old credit cards in good standing. Apply for new credit only when you are going to purchase an item of value, such as a house.

If your credit report consists only of credit card debt, a lower score will be reflected in your credit score. If, however, you have a diversified report, such as a mortgage and credit cards, your bills are paid on or before the due date and you have not gone over the forty-five percent rule, your credit score will reflect a higher score.

Your credit report determines your financial character, and creditors determine creditworthiness by this report. You can and should obtain a free credit report once a year. You can either obtain your credit report by going to www.annualcreditreport.com or by contacting the three credit reporting agencies. The credit report is free, although there is a fee to obtain your credit score.

According to the US PIRG Report of June 2004, "twenty-five percent of the credit reports surveyed contained serious errors. This could result in the denial of credit. Some credit reports contained personal contact information that was misspelled, outdated, belonged to a stranger, or information that was incorrect." Also, "twenty-two percent of the credit reports listed the same mortgage or loan twice. Almost eight percent of the credit reports were missing major credit, loan, mortgage, or other consumer accounts that demonstrate the creditworthiness of the consumer. Thirty percent of the credit reports contained credit accounts that had been closed by the consumer but remained listed as open. Over half of the credit reports surveyed contained either serious errors or others mistakes of some kind."

It is your money, and you should control your money as best as you can. An inaccurate credit report with adverse accounts can cost you money in the form of higher interest rates for loans. Why pay a higher interest rate for a mortgage if you can acquire the same mortgage at a lower rate of interest just by having an accurate and correct credit report? Most people have no idea what is on their credit report. With identify theft being in the forefront of the news, it is clear that anyone with computer knowledge can acquire your Social Security Number or credit card number and steal your identity and destroy your good credit.

Let's say you are applying for work at a bank as a loan officer. Their criteria for hiring could be a person who had no late payments in the last sixty days. You could be the most qualified person for the job, but you don't meet their criteria and will not be chosen for the job. It is very important to maintain an accurate and correct credit rating. You must know what is on your credit report. Now, let's take another twist in this scenario. What if you have good credit, but it is reported by credit agencies on your credit report that you have bad credit. Since you never looked at your credit report, you have no idea what the credit agencies are reporting. You applied for a car loan but you were denied. Now what? Will you do like most people and wonder why you were denied the car loan? Will you go to another dealership to apply for another loan? What will you do? Errors exist on the credit reports much of the time.

What is on your credit report?

_____
_____
_____
_____
_____
_____
_____
_____

Know your legal rights to obtain an accurate and correct credit report. You are protected by the Fair Credit Reporting Act, which I will summarize. For a complete copy of the Fair Credit Reporting Act, visit the Federal Trade Commission on the Internet at www.ftc.gov/os/statutes/031224fcra.pdf.

The summary of the Fair Credit Reporting Act states: "You have the right to obtain a free copy of your credit report once a year. You can also receive a free credit report if you have been unemployed and are currently seeking employment." You can pay for a credit report from all three agencies, as well. The cost is less than $10 for each report (charges for each state vary, so check the charges for your state).

The agencies are:

Equifax
P.O. Box 740241
Atlanta, GA 30374-0241

Trans Union
P.O. Box 1000
Chester, PA 19013

Experian
P.O. Box 2002
Allen, TX 75013

"You have the right to dispute any inaccurate information that is reported on your credit report." When you find an item on your report that is not correct, write the credit agency. Let the agency know the information and demand they remove the incorrect information from your report within forty-five days. Once the credit agency receives your letter, they will conduct an investigation. If their investigation cannot prove that the information is correct, they will remove it. If negative information is on your report and you don't know why it is there, request an investigation into that item.

"You have the right to request the credit agencies not to send credit information to you." Write all three credit agencies to request removal of your name from all marketing lists, mailing lists, and promotional lists. The credit agencies are in business to make money. They could sell your name to creditors or to those who create mailing lists and promotional lists. When you contact the credit agencies requesting an investigation, the agencies are required to contact you within forty-five days of the findings. If they don't contact you within the forty-five day period, they will have to take the information off your credit report.

You cannot correct your report if you don't know what is on the report. Therefore, to be assured that your credit report is accurate, order your credit report from all three agencies. Each credit-reporting agency keeps a separate file. In order to be informed about what each reporting agency is saying, you must order all three files.

When requesting a copy of your credit file, include a copy of a current utility bill to prove your name and current address. Also include a copy of your current driver's license. Send all letters by certified mail with a return receipt. A sample letter requesting a credit report is provided. Do not copy this letter; use it as a guideline to develop your personal letter.

A Sample Letter Requesting a Credit Report:

Address of the Credit Reporting Agency
City, State, Zip Code

Date

Your Name
Your Address
Your City, State, Zip Code
Your Date of Birth
Your Social Security Number

Dear Sirs:
Please send me my (name of agency) Credit Report. Enclosed are: a check for $9.00 to cover the cost of the credit report, a copy of my current driver's license to verify my date of birth, and a copy of my current utility bill to verify my current address.

I will look forward to receiving my credit report within two weeks.

Sincerely,
Your Full Name

It could take up to forty-five days to receive your credit report from the agency. If you don't receive your credit report within the timeline, notify them again, sending a copy of your return receipts along with a copy of the original letter sent requesting your report.

You may place a fraud alert on your credit report as a precaution or if you have been victimized. In order to start the process of protecting your credit identity, you must place a fraud alert in your credit file with all three credit-reporting agencies. This is an alert to the credit reporting agencies that no credit or change of address should be made to your file without your consent. When you put this alert on your credit file, the credit reporting agencies will notify you if anyone applies for credit in your name or tries to change your address or telephone number. The alert will stay in your file for ninety days. When placing a fraud alert in your file, include a copy of a current utility bill to prove your name and current address and a copy of your current driver's license. Send all letters by certified mail with a return receipt. A sample letter for requesting a fraud alert is provided. Do not copy this letter; instead, use it as a guideline to develop your own letter.

A Sample Letter Requesting a Fraud Alert:

Address of the Credit Reporting Agency
City, State, Zip Code

Your Name
Your Address
Your City, State, Zip Code
Your Date of Birth
Your Social Security Number
Your Credit Report File Number

Dear Sirs:
I am requesting that a fraud alert be placed on my credit report within 24 hours of receiving this request. Do not issue any credit reports to any lenders or other businesses without speaking to me directly. My home number is 212-222-3333. My cellular number is 212-333-8888. My business number is 212-555-4444. Please send me a copy of my credit report including the fraud alert.

Sincerely,
Your Full Name

If you have been victimized, it is best to place a security freeze on your credit file with all three credit reporting agencies. Placing a security freeze alert on your file will ensure that no one except you will be able to open a loan or establish credit in your name. In short, when a security freeze is placed on a file, lenders and other businesses will not have access to your file. Don't fret if you desire to open a new credit account; you will have access to a PIN and a specific process to follow to give you and the creditor access to your credit file. When placing a security freeze on your file, send all letters by certified mail with a return receipt. Include a copy of your police report concerning identity theft. Provide your driver's license and a current utility bill. Send to the following:

Equifax Security Freeze
P.O. Box 105788
Atlanta, GA 30348

Experian Security Freeze
P.O. Box 9554
Allen, TX 75013

Trans Union Security Freeze
P.O. Box 6790
Fullerton, CA 92834-6790

Once you have received your credit report, make one copy of each report. Check to ensure your name is spelled correctly, your address is correct, your Social Security Number is correct, and, in some cases, the last four digits of your SS# are correct. Check to ensure all creditors on your report are correct and all amounts owed are correct. Make notes in red ink of any errors on the copies. Check each report separately and completely.

Objectives of Chapter 3, Day 47:

- Ways to increase your credit score
- Ordering credit reports/fraud alerts/security freezes

Notes:

Day 48

A Sample Credit Report:

Personal Information	
John Doe	SSN: xxx-xxx-4678
Current Address	**Previous Address**
8910 Wise Street	123 Plain Street
Wisefield, USA 1234	Wisefield, USA 2468
You have been on our files since 12/1985	
Employment Data Reported	
Employer Name: APC Accounting, Inc.	**Position:** Accountant
2324 May Ave	
Wisefield, USA 1234	
Date Reported: 5/2003	
Account Information	
The information to the right helps explain the payment history contained in the accounts.	X=Unknown Ok=Current 30=Late 30 Days 60=Late 60 Days 90=Late 90 Days Days 120=Late 120 Days
Adverse Accounts	
American Express #5488853	Balance: $254.00
P.O. Box 1111	Date Verified 9/2004
American Express, USA 67891	High Balance: $100,000.00

A Sample Credit Report Cont:

	Credit Limit: $50,000.00
	30 – 60 – 90 – ok – ok – ok – 60 – 120 - ok
Satisfactory Accounts	
Bank of America	Balance: $0
P. O. Box 789	Date Verified: 9/2003
Bank of America, US 77335	High Balance: $1,000.00
	Credit Limit:
	$2,000.00
	ok – ok – ok – ok – ok – ok – ok – ok - ok
Regular Inquiries	
The following companies have received your credit report.	
Bank of America	
P. O. Box 789	
Bank of America, US 77335	
Requested ON: 5/2005	
Permissible Purpose: WRITTEN AUTHORIZATION	

Let's examine a credit report! Reading a credit report is different for each credit reporting agency. On each credit report, the headings and a legend indicate what the rank is for each creditor's item. In the sample credit report, the headings are self-explanatory and the legend is to the right of the section labeled Account Information. Read your credit reports and use the legend to assist you in identifying where you stand with your credit.

Only incorrect, inaccurate, or non-verifiable information can be removed legally from your credit report. If you were late making payments on an account for three months and the information is correct, accurate, and verifiable, it will remain on your credit report for up to seven years. Bankruptcies will remain on your credit report for up to ten years. Bankruptcy is not a death sentence. If you can start paying bills on time and show two years (sometimes sooner) of proof on your credit report that all bills were paid on time after the bankruptcy was discharged, you can purchase anything you desire, including a home.

Look at your adverse accounts on all three of your credit reports. Is all the information on your credit reports correct, accurate, or out of the seven year range? Look for inconsistencies. If any information on your credit report is inaccurate or incorrect, write a letter to the credit agency to challenge that item. However, if the information reported on your credit report is older than seven years and it is not a bankruptcy, you should request that the item be removed immediately.

It is your responsibility to keep accurate records of when you request the credit reporting agency to provide the proof and to follow up on all requests with proof that the request was made. A sample challenge letter is provided. Do not copy this letter. Use this letter as a guide to develop your own letter to send to the credit reporting agencies.

Notes:
_____
_____
_____
_____
_____
_____
_____

A Sample Challenge Letter:

Address of Credit Reporting Agency
City, State, Zip Code

Date
Your Name
Your Address
Your City, State, Zip Code
Your Date of Birth
Your Social Security Number
Your Credit Report File Number

Dear Sirs:

This letter is a formal complaint that you are reporting inaccurate and incorrect credit information. (List the information reported inaccurately, including the page number of the credit report.) This information is a mistake on either your part or the reporting creditor's part.

This information is to be deleted from my report as I have provided the proof of payments (attach proof). Also, send me an updated credit report showing the correction within forty-five days.

Sincerely,
Your Full Name

Notes:

Let's Look at the Adverse Account.

Adverse Accounts	
American Express #5488853	Balance: $254.00
P.O. Box 1111	Date Verified 9/2004
American Express, USA 67891	High Balance: $100,000.00
	Credit Limit: $50,000.00
	30 – 60 – 90 – ok – ok – ok – 60 – 120 - ok

Let's assume all the information in the Adverse Account is correct, accurate, and verifiable. How can the report be improved with these items remaining on the report?

_____
_____
_____

As a consumer, you must stay below forty-five percent of your credit limit (review Chapter 3, Day 47) to maintain a consistently high credit score. Pay all bills before they are due. If more credit is needed, simply call the company that issued the credit to request an increase in the credit limit. Never, ever go over your credit limit!

What is wrong with this Adverse Account?

_____
_____
_____

The Adverse Account payments have been late for 5 months, i.e., 30 – 60 – 90 – 60 – 120 days. The credit limit is only $50,000; however, the high balance was $100,000. Therefore, this person went over his/her credit limit. These issues will decrease the credit score.

What are inquirers? When you apply for new credit, companies view your credit report. This process is showed as a Regular Inquiry on your credit report.

Regular Inquiries	
The following companies have received your credit report.	
Bank Of America	
P. O. Box 789	
Bank of America, US 77335	
Requested ON: 5/2005	
Permissible Purpose: WRITTEN AUTHORIZATION	

A company must have your permission to view your credit report, and they must keep your permission on file. If you did not give permission for your credit report to be viewed, request that the creditor provide proof of your authorization. If the creditor cannot provide the proof, they will (at your request) write the credit agency and request that the inquiry be removed. Your current creditors have the right to review your credit file; this review will not hurt your credit score.

When in doubt, request that the credit reporting agency provide proof of any item on your credit report. The burden is on the credit reporting agency to provide proof that the information reported is correct.

Your road map to success: keep good records, order your credit report from all three credit reporting agencies, request that a fraud alert be placed on your credit file, validate each credit report received, and request correction of any incorrect or questionable information on your credit report.

Consistency is the key when challenging items on your credit report. It takes time. Don't get discouraged. Keep good records and follow up on the forty-sixth day with your proof. Follow up, follow up, and follow up!

Objectives of Chapter 3, Days 48:

- Read a credit report
- Challenge inaccurate information on your credit report

Notes:

Chapter 4

Your Largest Investment

Day 49

Home ownership could be the best investment and in most cases the biggest investment you can make. Why do I say home ownership could be the best investment? Structure! How you decide to structure the mortgage will make the difference. There are several types of mortgages, and each mortgage has its purpose. If you match the purpose to your personal goals, you will automatically select the correct mortgage. However, if you focus only on a low monthly payment, you may select the incorrect mortgage to reach your goal.

Let me share a story with you. I met a woman who wanted to purchase a home. She worked overtime on her job and saved enough money for a down payment on her dream home. Her goals were to live in her dream home until death, pay off her home, and upon her death, leave her dream home to her children. This woman is forty-five years young with a secure teaching position, and she does not plan to retire until the age of seventy-two. She went to her bank to speak with a loan officer. When good credit is established, acquire a mortgage from a bank.

Her loan officer advised her to secure an adjustable interest only mortgage. The adjustable interest only mortgage provided a low monthly payment with no equity and no systematic way to repay the mortgage in full. Is the adjustable interest only mortgage the best mortgage to meet her goals?

What type of mortgage may have been best for her to meet her goals? What were her goals? She wanted to live in her dream home for the duration of her life and pass her home on to her children. Would she want to stop paying for her home at some point? If the answer were "yes," a fixed rate mortgage would have served her better. Why? A fixed rate mortgage would have provided a systematic way to repay the mortgage in full and build equity in the home over time.

Her down payment and her ability to pay the higher monthly mortgage were adequate. All loan offices are not equal. Like any professional you hire, you need to find an honest person whom you trust to provide all the information you need. If you are not satisfied with the information they provide, walk away. You are the decision maker. The loan officer is working for you!

> When good credit is established, go to a bank to acquire a mortgage!

If you select the correct mortgage, you will be well on your way to creating wealth. Being a homebuyer is one of the fastest ways to accumulate money.

To select the correct mortgage, create your personal goal.

Do you want to pay off your home some day?
_____
_____
_____
_____
_____
_____

Would you like to build equity in your home?
_____
_____
_____
_____
_____
_____

Will you be moving in less than five years?
_____
_____
_____
_____
_____

What are your goals for your home?
_____
_____
_____
_____
_____
_____

Once your goals are established, match your goals to the specific type of mortgage and mortgage goal. These are some guidelines to follow when seeking a mortgage.

Guidelines:

Type of Mortgage	Mortgage Goals	Your Goals
Adjustable Rate	Short Term Mortgage	Live in home for three years or refinance in one to three years.
Fixed Rate	Long Term Mortgage	Consistent payments and systematic repayment.
No Down Payment	No down payment	Closing cost only and higher monthly payments.

You may be thinking of renting and not owning a home. Renters pay thousands of dollars just to live in an apartment or house that they will never own. Renters have no control over their rent payments. The landlord will create a lease. The landlord will determine all the amounts. The landlord can stipulate in the lease that the "Renter must move within sixty days if the property is sold." The renter has no choice! The landlord is the person who owns the property and is in charge, not the renter.

> Renters have no control over their monthly payment!

On average and over time, it is less expensive to own a home than it is to rent. Your home will increase in value. Also, you can deduct mortgage interest and taxes, and at some point in the future, your mortgage will be paid in full if you have a fixed rate mortgage. See the chart for a comparison of owning versus renting a home.

Cost of Ownership:

Home Owners	Cost	Benefits
Purchase a $350,000 house.	Down payment, Settlement cost, and Homeowner's Insurance.	1. Deduction on interest on the mortgage and property taxes. 2. Stop paying mortgage in 15-30 years.

Cost of Renting:

Home Owners	Cost	Benefits
Rent a $350,000 house.	First month's rent, last month's rent, and a security deposit.	NONE

As you can see from the above comparison, there are no benefits in renting. However, if you move every year or two, renting may be the best option for you. Why pay a down payment and settlement cost to purchase a home if you need to sell it in one year? Your options need to be mapped back to your personal goals.

Objectives of Chapter 4, Day 49:

- Selecting the correct mortgage for your needs
- Buying versus renting

Notes:

Chapter 5

Financial Fitness

Day 50

What does financial fitness mean? It means that if something should happen to you, will your family be taken care of at the same income level they are accustomed to or will they have to adjust to a lower income level?

As I travel and facilitate the Money Magnet workshops throughout the United States, I am introduced to many people who want to invest but are not financially fit to do so. Before you start to invest, ask yourself this question: am I financially fit to start the investment process?

_____
_____
_____
_____

How can I provide for my family when I am not around any longer?

_____
_____
_____
_____

By this time, you should be well on your way out of debt, achieving your life action plan, and almost ready to invest. If not, read this book and complete all the exercises before starting this section.

We will look at securing your family's future before investing by acquiring a Will, a Living Will, Life Insurance, Disability Insurance, a Living Trust, and Power of Attorney.

Every successful person has two things: an attorney and a financial coach. You will need the good advice of an attorney and a financial coach before you start investing.

They will work together to help you meet your investing and estate planning objectives.

What is a Will and who needs one? A Will is a legal document that states who receives ownership of your items, money, and your children when you die. A Will can be used to appoint a guardian to look after your children until they can look after themselves. A Will can save the expenses and possible disagreements that may arise when you die. Everyone should have a Will. A Will is the only way you can tell others how you want your assets to be distributed after your death. It is the only way you can provide for your family. If you only have a few assets, it is still worth making a Will so that you can ensure what happens to your assets and your family after you die. To create a Will, you will need to make an appointment with your attorney. If you decide not to make a Will, your state could determine what happens to your property, money, and your children.

What is a Living Will? It is a legal document that instructs your family and friends of your wishes if you should be on life-sustaining equipment. Would you want to live on life support or not? If you decide not to create a Living Will, you are relinquishing your decision to others who may not know exactly what you want. You should have this conversation with your medical doctor and then see your attorney to create your Living Will.

What is Life Insurance and how much is needed? Life Insurance ensures the financial stability of your family and loved ones if something should happen to you. How much money will it take annually for your family to sustain and maintain the same household? A good rule of thumb is 60-75% of your annual income.

_____
_____
_____
_____

How much money will it take annually for each child to attend college or to reach the age of 21? Add 4% per year for inflation.

_____
_____
_____
_____

How much total debt do you owe?

_____
_____
_____
_____

How much money do you owe on your mortgage?

_____
_____
_____
_____

What is the estimate of your funeral expense? (Contact a funeral director in your area to obtain an estimate.) You could preplan your funeral arrangements. This will take the burden off your family in their time of bereavement; also, you could lock in the cost at today's prices.

_____
_____
_____
_____

How much will it cost to settle your estate? You can get an estimate from your attorney.

_____
_____
_____
_____

How much savings and retirement funds are accumulated to date?

_____
_____
_____
_____

Basically, you should add up all your expenses (the first six questions) and subtract your savings and retirement. This process should give you an estimate of how much insurance to purchase. When complete, contact a competent insurance agent. You may want to ask your friends and family members for recommendations of a good insurance agent.

What is Disability Insurance? Disability Insurance replaces a portion of your income when you are unable to work because of injury or illness. Your employer may provide long-term and short-tem disability insurance for you. Check with your employer to see how you may participate in their program.

What is a Living Trust? A Living Trust is a legal document to assist in the settlement of your estate. You may set it up to be revocable or irrevocable. A Living Trust transfers property to responsible person, a trustee, who holds the property for the benefit of a beneficiary (this could be your children). See your attorney to create a Living Trust.

What is a Power of Attorney? This is a legal document to transfer your legal and financial decisions to someone of your choice if you are disabled and unable to carry out your financial obligations. Your attorney can help you create a Power of Attorney.

Notes:

_____
_____
_____

Once you start reducing your bad debt and your high-interest savings account is building, you can utilize 50% of your savings from this account to start your investment plan. You can also use your money from increasing your cash flow (review Chapter 2 and Chapter 3).

Before you invest, you should know several things. Don't put all of your hard-earned dollars in one type of investment. It would be foolish to invest all of your money in one company. If they go bankrupt, you will lose all of your money. Have a good mix of investments in your portfolio. Every investment has some level of risk. There is always a chance that you will lose all or part of your money.

Determine if you are a long-term investor or a short-term investor. A long-term investor is very conservative. The longer the investment, the greater the reward, and the risk is minimized. Long-term investments are for five or more years. A short-term investor is a risk taker. They will take money in and out of investments, trying to make lots of money in a short period of time. Review Day 8: Different Money Styles.

History indicates that the most secure way to make money is over the long term. Whatever type of investor you happen to be, do not put your money at risk until you have reached financial fitness, which is achieved by reducing debt, acquiring your Fallback Money, and utilizing your high-interest savings along with your increased cash flow to start your investment program and security for your family. If you are not ready to invest just yet, learn as much as you can about investing and investments.

Notes:

_____
_____
_____

Testimonials

Oh sure, we knew that we were choking in the debt of living. We knew that as Christians, it was our obligation as good stewards to owe no one and to have to give, but how could that be achieved today? Today, when it takes two people working in a household to even maintain the household at just above the poverty level? Today, when retired folk go back to work just to afford the cost of medication?

Do we borrow? Do we consolidate? Do we just work until we physically cannot work any longer?

What about our obligation to our church? How do we give out tithes and make it when we barely have enough for us?

As a family, we do share the cheers and the fears. But it all came into place when my sister said, "I know a lady, Denise Scott, who has really been helping people in a miraculous way. I know you did not ask for a loan, but I would be willing to pay for you to consult with her because when we learn together, we can break a generation of spending and leave a legacy of good stewardship skills for generations to come."

So that is how we began the journey to freedom.

Being an outdoors person, I was thrilled at the adventure. My husband, being a city boy, was a little more cautious. Yeah, he could look up the road and see the magnificent view, but he wondered if just off the path there were lions or tigers or bears. In spite of all the trepidation, we began with Denise as our guide.

Many times, I wanted to run ahead, and my husband just wanted to sit and rest. Many times, I wanted to try all the fruits and berries along the road, and my husband had to study them before even trying the tiniest bite. Sometimes I got so frustrated I just shook my head, stuffed my hands in my pockets, and stomped down the road. A lot of times, my husband would even have the nerve to go back to a turn in the road to check the direction while I waited for him impatiently, tapping my foot in disgust. The consistency was our guide, Denise Scott.

Are we there yet? No, but we know we will get there. No more do you hear, "Are we there yet?" We don't panic and breathe into the paper bag when we are asked by our guide such things as "Did you cut up all your credit cards?" and "How are you managing Christmas giving this year?" Instead, we appreciate the incentive of spending the monthly "fun money" and anticipate our savings growing.

No, we are not there yet, but we have a steady, even pace, and we are all on the same road with plenty of time to stop and enjoy the magnificent view of financial freedom. We truly know how the Israelites must have felt as they looked down on the promised land after 40 years of wandering.

Thank you, Denise Scott — for your wisdom, your patience, your sense of humor, and not giving up on us. You are blessed because you are a blessing. You have taught us the skills to perform our fiduciary duty as the hands and feet of Christ to receive so that we can give.

Sincerely,
The Johnstons
Ohio

I would like to just give a little thanks to Money Magnet, Inc. and Denise. She has given me financial guidance that has let me live a stress-free life. I met Denise two years after 9/11 after being unemployed for two years. I had nowhere to turn. I found Money Magnet, Inc. and gave Denise a call. She took my information gave me suggestions for my present situation.

She took a good look at my situation and told me how I could get my ducks in a row and get on the positive side of things. I heard from her two weeks later, and she gave me a game plan that would get my credit score well over 700 FICO in a matter of 90 days. Since that time, I have had banks trying to give loans beyond my wildest dreams. This has been a dream come true for me.

I stay in touch with Denise as a friend as well as a financial advisor for my finances in general as well as all of my investments.

Regards,
Thomas Hunt
Connecticut

I've been shocked, which is a good thing, about how doable these steps are.

Sincerely,
Carolyn Dentz
Dentz Design
New Jersey

Epilogue

A high school drop out, Denise Scott found herself divorced and $20,000 in debt in the late 1980s. What she did was acknowledge her situation and then vow to improve her personal financial outlook. Now, she's the chief financial officer of the Brookhaven-based financial wellness corporation, Money Magnet, Inc., and the author of her soon-to-be-published book, *How To Be A Money Magnet*.

Scott was born and raised in Chester, where she dropped out of Chester High School in 1973 as a senior. Having come from a family of musicians, she had a music scholarship for playing the piano, but she lacked the passion for it. She found herself doing many jobs, such as pumping gas and being a nursing assistant.

However, she found it hard to pay the bills, so she decided to go back to school. "I guess that I couldn't find a job past minimum wage," Scott said.

She was accepted into Widener University as a special student, planning to take one class at a time. Her first class, one on college technique, cost $15. "I had $15," Scott said. "I started down the path." At first, she started in business administration, but that eventually changed to information technology.

Then, in the late 1980s, she became divorced and acquired $20,000 in debt from five credit cards, her car loan, and her mortgage. "When you have someone else paying your bills, you don't think about it," she said. "That brought me clarity."

She accepted her position and made a commitment to herself. "How can I get myself out of debt?" So she devised her plan. "I stopped using credit cards," Scott said, adding that she called her credit card companies, asked for a lower interest rate, and received it. Four years later, she reached her goal. Then she made another promise. "I will never be in credit card debt again," Scott said. "If I can't pay it in 30, 60, or 90 days, I don't use it."

After eliminating her debt, she started to save money and progressed into investing in real estate and the stock market. In 2002, she opened Money Magnet, Inc. "If I can become debt free and financially free, everyone who desires the same and is willing to do the work required can accomplish the same goal. It is a matter of your will."

If you take care of the money that comes to you, more money will follow. Money attracts more money!

An excerpt published by Delaware County Daily Times on Thursday, May 31, 2007

Thank You

I hope you enjoyed reading this book as much as I enjoyed writing it. It has been my pleasure to share the practical techniques to financial freedom with you. One more recommendation: spend 50% of your tax return. Save the other portion in your high-interest savings account. Everyone who desires to achieve a higher level of financial freedom can do so by applying these easy steps in this book. Feel free to send your testimonials to info@moneymagnetinc.com.

Appendix

Completed Life Action Plan:

Start Date	**Goal:** Sell my condominium in six months.	Scheduled Completion Date	Actual Completion Date
	Small Daily Tasks		
6/5	-Self assessment of home	6/5	6/5
6/6	- Evaluate what items need to be fixed or upgraded in home	6/6	6/6
6/7	-Living Room	6/7	6/7
6/8	-Dining Room	6/8	6/8
6/11	-Kitchen	6/11	6/11
6/12	-Bathroom	6/12	6/12
6/13	-Bedroom	6/13	6/13
6/14	Hallway	6/14	6/14
6/15	Laundry Room	6/15	6/15

Completed Life Action Plan Cont'd:

6/15	Hire home inspector to evaluate the interior and exterior of the home.	6/15	6/15
6/19	Inspection	6/19	6/19
6/19	Pay inspector	6/19	6/19
6/21-6/29	Fix items based on the recommendations of the inspector.	6/29	6/29
7/2 – 7/3	Hire painter to paint the interior of the home a neutral color	7/3	7/3
7/9	- Prepare Bedroom to be painted	7/9	7/9
7/9	- Prepare Laundry Room to be painted	7/9	7/9
7/9	- Prepare Hallway to be painted	7/9	7/9
7/9	- Prepare Bathroom to be painted	7/9	7/9

Completed Life Action Plan Cont'd:

7/10	Painter to paint Bedroom, Laundry, Hallway, and Bathroom.	7/10	7/10
7/10	- Prepare Dinning Room to be painted.	7/10	7/10
7/10	- Prepare Kitchen to be painted.	7/10	7/10
7/10	-Prepare Living Room to be painted.	7/10	7/10
7/11	Painter to paint Dinning Room, Kitchen, and Living Room.	7/11	7/11
7/11	Pay painter	7/11	7/11
7/12	Hire a carpet cleaning service to clean all wall-to-wall carpet in the home.	7/12	7/12
7/16	Carpet to be cleaned.	7/16	7/16
7/16	Pay for carpet cleaning service.	7/16	7/16
7/17	Hire an appraiser to evaluate the value of the home.	7/17	7/17
7/18	Home appraised	7/18	7/18
7/18	Pay appraiser	7/18	7/18

Completed Life Action Plan Cont'd:

7/19	Set price for home based on appraiser's recommendations.	7/19	7/19
7/23	Create a sales sheet with pictures of the home and "Must Sell" as the caption.	7/23	7/23
7/24	Place sales sheet with pictures on local billboards.	7/24	7/24
7/25	Place advertisement in local paper.	7/25	7/25
7/26	Place advertisement on the Internet.	7/26	7/26
7/27	Place an oversized sales sign in front of home.	7/27	7/27
7/30	Set time and date for an open house.	7/30	7/30
8/12	Open house.	8/12	8/12
10/31	If home does not sell within three months, place home up for auction.	10/31	10/31

Life Action Plan:

Start Date	Goal:	Scheduled Completion Date	Actual Completion Date

Life Action Plan:

Start Date	Goal:	Scheduled Completion Date	Actual Completion Date

Life Action Plan:

Start Date	Goal:	Scheduled Completion Date	Actual Completion Date

Completed Example 1: Goal with Tasks:

Start Date	**Goal:** Sell my condominium in six months.	Scheduled Completion Date	Actual Completion Date
	Small Daily Tasks		
	-Self assessment of home		
	-Evaluate what items need to be fixed or upgraded in home		
	-Living Room		
	-Dining Room		
	-Kitchen		
	-Bathroom		
	-Bedroom		
	Hallway		
	Laundry Room		

Completed Example 1: Goal with Tasks Cont'd:

	Hire home inspector to evaluate the interior and exterior of the home.		
	Inspection		
	Pay inspector		
	Fix items based on the recommendations of the inspector.		
	Hire painter to paint the interior of the home a neutral color		
	-Prepare Bedroom to be painted		
	-Prepare Laundry Room to be painted		
	-Prepare Hallway to be painted		
	-Prepare Bathroom to be painted		

Completed Example 1: Goal with Tasks Cont'd:

	Painter to paint Bedroom, Laundry, Hallway, and Bathroom.		
	-Prepare Dinning Room to be painted.		
	-Prepare Kitchen to be painted.		
	-Prepare Living Room to be painted.		
	Painter to paint Dinning Room, Kitchen, and Living Room.		
	Pay painter		
	Hire a carpet cleaning Service to clean all wall-to-wall carpet in the home.		
	Carpet to be cleaned.		
	Pay for carpet cleaning service.		
	Hire an appraiser to evaluate the value of the home.		
	Home appraised		
	Pay appraiser		

Completed Example 1: Goal with Tasks Cont'd:

	Set price for home based on appraiser's recommendations.		
	Create a sales sheet with pictures of the home and "Must Sell" as the caption.		
	Place sales sheet with pictures on local billboards.		
	Place advertisement in local paper.		
	Place advertisement on the Internet.		
	Place an oversized sales sign in front of home.		
	Set time and date for an open house.		
	Open house.		
	If home does not sell with in three months place home up for auction.		

References

Creditcards.com Credit Card Industry Facts and Personal Debt Statistics. www.creditcards.com.

Edmunds.com Tips and Advice. www.edmunds.com.

Federal Trade Commission. Fair Credit Reporting Act. ftc.gov/os/statutes/031224fcra.pdf.

Rector, Robert and Johnson, Kirk, Ph.D. Understanding Poverty in America. www.heritage.org.

Taylor, Shelley, Peplau, Letitia, and Sears, David. Social Psychology 12th Edition. Upper Saddle River: New Jersey 2006.

US PIRG Report. Mistakes Do Happen: A Look at Errors in Consumer Credit Reports. June 2004. www.static.uspirg.org.

Notes